Taylor Swift - Shake it Off:

Standing Tall and Staying Real in a Shaky World – 34 Qualities That Shaped Taylor Swift's Life

Scarlett Smith

Ella Sophie

Contents

Copyright

Taylor Swift - Shake it Off : Standing Tall and Staying Real in a Shaky World – 34 Qualities That Shaped Taylor Swift's Life

Copyright © 2023 by Scarlett Smith & Ella Sophie

Introduction

Dear Reader,

There's a magical quality about the music and persona of Taylor Swift. It's as if her songs, filled with stories of love, loss, triumph, and resilience, become the soundtrack to our lives, resonating deeply with each one of us.

But have you ever wondered about the woman behind the lyrics? The journey of the girl who, equipped with a guitar and a dream, became an inspiration to millions around the world? That's the story you're about to dive into.

This isn't just a chronicle of Taylor's rise to superstardom; it's a deeply personal, immersive experience that unveils the woman behind the music. We will delve into her earliest years, the initial spark of her talent, and the daunting move from Pennsylvania to Nashville that launched her meteoric rise.

Witness the determination, courage, and resilience Taylor demonstrated in her path towards global recognition. We go beyond the stage and the red carpet events, into the intimate spaces of her life – her fears, her dreams, the relationships that shaped her, and her unyielding bond with her fans.

Expect the unexpected as we journey through her transformation from a young country artist into an international pop sensation, a journey dotted with challenges and triumphs, criticisms, and praises.

And finally, we will discover how Taylor continues to shake off the pressure, standing tall and staying real in an ever-shaky world, transforming negatives into positives – a life lesson we could all draw inspiration from.

Get ready to witness the story of Taylor Swift as never before. As you turn each page, you're sure to find something that will make you admire her even more, something that will make you fall in love with her music all over again. Let's begin this journey.

Chapter 1

A Star is Born – The Early Years Of Taylor Swift

Once upon a winter's day, on December 13, 1989, in the quiet town of Reading, Pennsylvania, a star was born. Her name? Taylor Alison Swift. Daughter to Andrea and Scott Swift, her story starts as an ordinary girl in a small town, but as we know, Taylor's journey was destined to be anything but ordinary.

From a very young age, Taylor was enraptured by music. At just six years old, she became fascinated with Disney songs, particularly the one from "The Little Mermaid". In a 2009 interview with The New Yorker, she shared, "It was the story-telling through music...making a narrative that made me fall in love with music." This love was not just a childhood fancy, but a passion that would shape her life and career.

Taylor was different, and this difference sometimes made fitting in with peers at school challenging. But, as Swift shared in a VH1 Storytellers session in 2012, "I remember writing songs in my bedroom instead of going to parties." This dedication, this willingness to 'shake it off' and choose her path, proved pivotal in her journey.

When Taylor was 14, her family moved to Hendersonville, Tennessee to support her dream of pursuing country music. The relocation proved a significant leap toward the bright lights of the music industry. As she revealed in a Rolling Stone interview from 2010, "My parents knew my dreams and understood them enough to help me chase them. I'm forever grateful for that."

Despite the limelight, fame, and critical acclaim that came her way, Taylor remained true to her roots. As she shared in her acceptance speech at the 2016 Grammy Awards, "There are going to be people along the way who will try to undercut your success... But if you just focus on the work... you will know that it was you and the people who love you who put you there. And that will be the greatest feeling in the world."

This chapter reflects the early years of Taylor Swift, from her birth to her first steps into the music industry. It was a time of learning, dreaming, and preparing for a journey that would take her far beyond the borders of Reading, Pennsylvania.

In conclusion, Taylor's early years were an amalgamation of dreams, challenges, passion, and most importantly, resilience. Despite the pressures of fitting in, she chose her own unique path, shaking off societal expectations, thus embodying the principle that underpins our narrative - standing tall and staying real in a shaky world.

As we step into the subsequent chapters of Taylor's life, remember this initial lesson. Taylor Swift teaches us that staying true to oneself, pursuing our dreams relentlessly, and being prepared to 'shake off' the negativity are keys to standing tall and staying real, just like she did, and continues to do so. Her journey teaches us the importance of authenticity and resilience in pursuing our dreams - a fitting start to our exploration of the 'Shake It Off – The Taylor Swift Way of

Standing Tall and Staying Real in a Shaky World - 34 Powerful Principles'.

Chapter 2

From Pennsylvania to Nashville: The Big Move

In the scenic countryside of Pennsylvania, amidst rows of Christmas trees, a young Taylor Swift discovered her love for music. But to nurture her talent, she needed to take a leap of faith and embark on an extraordinary journey. It was a journey that would take her from her comfortable childhood home to the heart of America's country music scene - Nashville, Tennessee.

At the tender age of 14, Taylor and her family made the bold decision to move to Nashville, a city they barely knew, driven by nothing more than a shared dream and unshakeable faith. It was a significant moment, as Swift recalled in an interview with CMT in 2006, "It was a huge decision for my family to move from Pennsylvania, but we all knew that if I wanted to have a chance in country music, Nashville was the place to be."

And so, the Swifts packed their lives into boxes, leaving behind familiar faces and surroundings. The family's selfless act of relocating for the sake of Taylor's dream speaks volumes about their support for her ambition. As Swift reflected in a 2010 interview with Seventeen, "I'm incredibly lucky that my family was ready to make sacrifices for my career. I never forget that."

But Taylor's first steps into Nashville weren't smooth sailing. It was a big pond, and she was a small fish. To carve her niche, Swift had to network, write songs, and make demo tapes to attract the attention of record labels. In her acceptance speech at the 2013 Billboard Music Awards, Taylor mentioned, "You've got to work hard and make things happen for yourself."

The hard work paid off when Swift caught the eye of Scott Borchetta, an executive at the fledgling Big Machine Records. Taylor became one of the first signings to the label, a decisive moment in her career. The young artist, full of dreams and determination, finally had the chance to turn her dreams into reality.

Swift didn't waste any time. By 2006, she was ready to release her self-titled debut album, a collection of songs she had written during her early days in Nashville. The success of this album confirmed that Swift's bold move had been worth it. Reflecting on this in an interview with Rolling Stone in 2009, she said, "I've always strived to be successful, not famous."

Despite the success, Taylor's heart remained firmly grounded. She never lost her humility or her connection with her fans, which she attributes to her small-town upbringing and the life-changing move to Nashville. She said in an interview with Vogue in 2012, "Moving to Nashville taught me everything I needed to know about being an artist, not just a singer. It's about more than just standing on stage and singing. It's about connecting with people."

To wrap up this chapter, Taylor Swift's move from Pennsylvania to Nashville is a powerful testament to her courage, dedication, and the unwavering support of her family. It reinforces a principle that underpins our narrative – standing tall and staying real in a shaky world.

As we continue to explore the 'Shake It Off – The Taylor Swift Way of Standing Tall and Staying Real in a Shaky World - 34 Powerful Principles', remember this lesson: Having the courage to pursue your dreams, even if it means taking a significant risk, can lead to extraordinary outcomes. Like Taylor, let's embrace the big moves in our lives as opportunities for growth, always staying true to ourselves.

Chapter 3

Recognizing Talent: The Spark that Ignited a Flame

There's a fine line between having a dream and making that dream a reality. For Taylor Swift, the spark that bridged that gap was recognition – recognition from the right people who saw the potential in a young girl with a guitar and a heart full of stories.

Swift's family's move to Nashville marked the beginning of her journey into the music industry. But it was when Scott Borchetta of Big Machine Records recognized her talent that her musical aspirations began to take flight. According to an interview with CMT in 2006, Taylor stated, "Scott saw something in me that I always knew was there, but that no one had taken the chance to see before."

However, it wasn't just industry bigwigs who noticed Taylor's talent. She also quickly became a fan favorite. Her emotional honesty, relatable lyrics, and infectious melodies resonated with listeners worldwide. Her debut album, "Taylor Swift", released in 2006, was met with overwhelming success and propelled her into the limelight. Swift has always acknowledged the critical role her fans have played in her journey. At the 2014 American

Music Awards, she confessed, "To the fans who have made my life a dream, I love you with all my heart."

Yet, Swift's rise to fame didn't stop her from being true to herself. Her integrity, authenticity, and courage remained intact, even as her life transformed. In an interview with Vanity Fair in 2013, Swift shared, "I don't let fame define me. I define myself."

She used her platform not just to share her music but also to inspire, support, and stand up for those who needed it. In her acceptance speech at the 2016 Grammys, Swift empowered young women worldwide with her words, "There will be people along the way who will try to undercut your success...but if you just focus on the work and you don't let those people sidetrack you you'll look around, and you will know that you put yourself there, and that will be the greatest feeling in the world."

Swift's tale, from her early recognition to her global success, teaches us that one spark can indeed ignite a flame. She did not just rest on the laurels of her recognition but instead used it as fuel to work harder and reach higher, all while staying grounded and true to herself.

Wrapping up this chapter, Taylor Swift's journey illustrates a pivotal principle of our narrative - recognizing your talent and using it as a stepping stone towards achieving your dreams, all while staying real and grounded in a world that often sways with the winds of fame and success.

As we continue unfolding the 'Shake It Off – The Taylor Swift Way of Standing Tall and Staying Real in a Shaky World - 34 Powerful Principles', let us remember this learning: Recognize your talent, pursue your dreams, and make your mark, just like Taylor did. Despite all, never lose sight of who you truly are.

That's the Taylor Swift way of shaking it off and standing tall in a shaky world.

Chapter 4

First Strums - Learning to Play the Guitar

A twelve-string guitar, a girl with a dream, and a journey of a thousand miles that began with a single strum. This, dear readers, is the tale of how Taylor Swift fell in love with the guitar.

It was during her early years in Pennsylvania that a computer repairman named Ronnie Cremer introduced her to the world of chords and strums. Cremer, spotting a guitar lying in the corner of the Swift household, offered to teach Taylor some basics, a decision that would become a pivotal moment in her journey.

In an interview with "60 Minutes" in 2011, Swift said, "The moment I could play a chord, I was writing songs. I was writing about what was happening to me right then and there." It was as if the guitar became her confidante, her diary - a friend she could share her deepest thoughts with.

But learning the guitar was not a walk in the park. Swift was challenged, but she shook it off and persevered. In her acceptance speech at the Academy of Country Music Awards in 2011, Swift acknowledged, "This is the first time that I've ever accepted an award on national television, and I want to say to

Ronnie Cremer, 'Thank you for teaching me to play guitar.' You have changed my life."

Swift's commitment to the guitar was no passing fancy but a burning passion. As she grew in her musical journey, she became recognized for her unique guitar-playing style. It became synonymous with her performances - from the small stages of Nashville to the grandeur of the Grammy Awards.

Despite her fame, Swift always kept her gratitude towards her early mentor, Ronnie Cremer. Her story shows us the power of an open heart, of passion, and of how learning a new skill can ignite a spark that can change your life.

Wrapping up this chapter, it's clear that Taylor Swift's journey with the guitar wasn't just about music; it was about resilience, dedication, and the ability to 'shake it off' in the face of challenges. This is yet another inspiring principle in our exploration of the 'Shake It Off – The Taylor Swift Way of Standing Tall and Staying Real in a Shaky World - 34 Powerful Principles'.

As we continue our journey through Taylor's life, remember this: Each one of us has our 'guitar' – a passion that defines us and makes us who we are. And when we stumble upon it, it's our duty to nurture it, to learn and grow with it, and let it guide us to our true calling, just like Taylor did.

With guitar in hand, Taylor Swift began to express herself through melodies and lyrics that would soon resonate with millions. Her songwriting, an intrinsic part of her music and her identity, was often her way of navigating the world around her. She once confessed in a Rolling Stone interview in 2012, "I've been careful in love, but careless in songs. Because they're where I can be reckless."

The young Taylor, fearless and full of dreams, started to perform at local venues, festivals, and fairs around her new home in Nashville. Each performance, each strum on her guitar, was a step closer to the world she aspired to be part of. But, as she shared during her concert at Madison Square Garden in 2011, "It was a lot of hard work, and there were times when I doubted if we were ever going to make it, but we kept going."

Swift's determination to play the guitar and write her own songs indeed set her apart. It gave her the power to speak her truth and connect with people across the globe on a deeply personal level. Her courage and resolve to shape her narrative through her music and her guitar became one of the many reasons why she could shake off the doubts and criticisms.

Chapter 5

First Words - Discovering Her Gift for Songwriting

Taylor Swift didn't just strum her first chords on a guitar; she also found a unique voice that would eventually echo across the globe. Her songwriting, a natural extension of her love for storytelling, is one of the many gifts that set her apart in the music industry.

From her very first songs, Taylor proved to have a unique knack for storytelling. This talent didn't go unnoticed. In fact, at age 14, she became the youngest songwriter ever hired by the Sony/ATV Music publishing house. This early recognition highlighted the extraordinary talent of a young girl from Pennsylvania, making her dreams seem all the more attainable.

In an interview with Elle Magazine in 2019, Taylor shared, "I wrote my first song when I was 12 years old, and it was about this boy who liked another girl. The song was my way of dealing with it. Songwriting has always been my way of understanding myself and the world around me." Her songs, filled with personal experiences and raw emotions, have been her refuge, her strength, and her connection to her fans.

As we dive into the lyrics of her early songs, we see a young woman navigating her way through life, love, and everything in between. Her song "Tim McGraw," for instance, evokes a sense of nostalgia, a tribute to young love, and a sign of things to come. As Taylor said at her debut album release party in 2006, "I wrote the song in my freshman year of high school. It's about just knowing that you're going to have to leave something behind, but you'll have good memories."

This extraordinary ability to connect with people's experiences and emotions was evident in her debut album, "Taylor Swift," which swiftly climbed the charts and won the hearts of millions. The girl with a guitar and a story had now become a voice of her generation.

In conclusion, Chapter 5, Unravels Taylor Swift's unique gift of songwriting. Her talent for transforming personal experiences into relatable narratives and emotive songs has empowered her to stand tall in a shaky world. This ability has allowed her to shake off criticisms and remain genuine, offering a vital lesson in authenticity, resilience, and emotional intelligence.

To explore the journey of Taylor Swift, remember this - embracing our unique gifts, much like Taylor embraced her songwriting, can empower us to stay real and stand tall, regardless of how shaky the world gets. This is just another example of how Taylor Swift exemplifies the principles we are exploring in 'Shake it Off – The Taylor Swift Way Of Standing Tall and Staying Real in a Shaky World'.

Particularly during her teen years, Taylor was extremely perceptive of the emotions swirling around her, using these as inspiration. She transformed her observations into meaningful, relatable lyrics, pouring her heart out into her songs. This lyrical honesty is a significant reason for her immense popularity; listeners across the world found a piece of their stories in her songs.

"There's a special place in my heart for the ones who were with me from the very beginning," Taylor told fans in a 2015 Tumblr post. True to her words, her songs often bear a personal and nostalgic tone that bonds her with her fans, making her music a shared journey rather than a one-way communication.

A fascinating aspect of Taylor's songwriting journey was her incredible work ethic. Just like with her guitar, she practiced her craft constantly, striving to improve. She once revealed in a Rolling Stone interview in 2014, "I wrote songs in my notebook instead of paying attention in class. I'd stay up late and wake up early. It was an obsession."

This diligence has resulted in a plethora of chart-topping hits, each carrying the distinctive Taylor Swift signature of raw emotion and captivating storytelling. She created her own narrative, shaping her image through her songs. Taylor was not just a singer; she was a storyteller, an artist painting vivid pictures through her music.

Chapter 6

Fearless - Overcoming Stage Fright and Stepping into the Limelight

There's something enchanting about Taylor Swift on stage, her sparkling eyes filled with a mix of excitement and gratitude, her energetic performances captivating thousands. It's a sight that fills the heart of every Swiftie with joy. But did you know that stepping into the limelight wasn't always easy for Taylor?

Even the most shining stars experience their share of shadows. Young Taylor was no exception. She had to overcome one significant hurdle before she could fully embrace her destiny: stage fright. She told MTV News in 2009, "I remember when I was in fourth grade... I got up to sing the national anthem at a basketball game, and I completely choked. I forgot the words and ran off the court crying."

But just like in her songs, Taylor faced her fears head-on. She was determined to shake off her stage fright. She understood that in order to touch people with her music, she needed to be brave enough to share it.

And so, she practiced relentlessly. She performed at local events and contests, open mics, and even at a cafe near her home. Her motto, as she expressed at a 2014 press conference, was "You have to be Fearless to have success." She found that the more she exposed herself to the stage, the easier it became.

With every performance, her confidence grew, and the stage began to feel like a second home. She learnt to feed off the energy of her audience, and her stage fright gradually transformed into stage thrill. This thrilling connection between her and her fans is palpable in her performances. During her 2014 iHeartRadio Music Festival performance, she shared, "I look out into the audience and I see a bunch of wide eyes and kind hearts... that's why I do this."

In time, Taylor became a commanding presence on stage, her performances a spectacle of lights, emotions, and music that leaves the audience mesmerized. She stands tall, fearless, and real, shaking off any remnant of fear, completely embracing her passion.

When Taylor was only 11, she had her first major performance at The Bluebird Cafe in Nashville, a venue known for launching many successful country music careers. The weight of this opportunity was not lost on her. In a candid interview with CMT in 2006, Taylor said, "It was nerve-wracking. I was about to play my guitar and sing songs I'd written in front of people who could make my dreams come true."

However, once she started strumming her guitar and singing her heart out, she realized that all eyes were on her, not to scrutinize, but to appreciate her talent. It was at this moment that Taylor understood the unique magic of live performances – the energy, the interaction, the raw, undeniable connection. She shook off her stage fright, replacing it with excitement and a sense of purpose.

One particular memory stood out from this period. Taylor spoke about it at the 2013 Billboard Music Awards, "I was 16, and I was singing a song on an awards show. I was so excited because my parents were in the audience. I saw a glimmer of pride in their eyes. At that moment, I knew I'd conquered my fear. It wasn't about me being scared anymore. It was about sharing my music, my stories."

To conclude, delves into Taylor's journey of overcoming stage fright and stepping into the limelight. Her courage in facing her fears, her resilience in continuously pushing her boundaries, and her determination to connect with her fans reflect her fearless spirit. It's a testament to the principle that being real and standing tall often means confronting our fears, shaking them off, and turning them into stepping stones towards our dreams.

As we move forward in our exploration of 'Shake It Off – The Taylor Swift Way Of Standing Tall and Staying Real in a Shaky World - 34 Powerful Principles', let's remember this lesson from Taylor's journey. It's about confronting fears, shaking off doubts, and being fearless in the pursuit of what sets our soul on fire. Taylor Swift's way is not just about succeeding, but about fearlessly embracing the journey, about standing tall, and staying real.

Chapter 7

Rise to Stardom: The Breakthrough Album

In 2006, Taylor Swift introduced herself to the world. At only 16 years old, she released her debut, self-titled album, "Taylor Swift," a collection of songs she started writing at the tender age of 12. While she was already a known face in Nashville, the album was her grand entrance to the global music stage.

She once said in an interview with Oprah Winfrey in 2009, "I wrote every song on my debut album. It's a diary of my early teens. It's raw, it's real, and it's mine. It's an open letter to the world." This confession laid the foundation for Taylor's approach to music—honest, emotive, and unmistakably hers.

The world embraced Taylor with open arms. Her debut album peaked at number five on the Billboard 200 and spent 275 weeks on the chart, a record for a female artist at that time. However, it was the song "Love Story," a single from her second album "Fearless," that made her a household name. Inspired by the narrative of Romeo and Juliet, Taylor wrote the song as a response to her parents' concerns about her young love. The song quickly became an anthem for teenage romance.

She shared at the 2008 American Music Awards, "I remember the night I wrote 'Love Story.' I felt so strongly about what I wanted to say, about wanting to write a love story with a better ending. And to see people sing it back to me years later... it's magical. It's the best kind of connection."

That connection was felt by millions. Taylor Swift was no longer just a talented newcomer; she was a global superstar. Yet, despite the sudden influx of fame, Taylor stayed grounded, and she shook off any pressure that came with stardom.

She stated in her 2020 Netflix documentary, 'Miss Americana': "I've learned over the years that it's not about being perfect or meeting everyone's expectations. It's about staying true to who I am, about telling my stories."

Picking up where we left off, Taylor's breakthrough wasn't just marked by her commercial success, but her recognition within the industry. It was with this album that she started collecting her first major music awards, validating her talents in front of the world.

She scored her first Country Music Association (CMA) award for Horizon Award in 2007, an honor bestowed upon rising stars. This win was significant, not just for Taylor, but for the industry as well. She was the youngest artist to ever win that award.

Taylor once commented on her early success during a back-stage interview at the 2007 CMA Awards, "I've dreamt about what it would be like to maybe win one of these someday, but I never actually thought it would happen. I'm so thankful to everyone who made this dream come true."

That dream became even bigger with her second album, "Fearless," released in 2008. It won Album of the Year at the 2009 CMA Awards, making Taylor, at age 20, the youngest artist to win the prestigious award, and the first female solo country artist to do so. "Fearless" also earned her first Grammy for Album of the Year in 2010, again making history as the youngest recipient of the award.

However, the road to success wasn't without bumps. The infamous incident at the 2009 MTV Video Music Awards, where Kanye West interrupted her acceptance speech, could have shaken her confidence. But in true Taylor fashion, she shook it off. As she said later in a 2019 interview with Rolling Stone, "It taught me to separate my public and personal life, that I have the right to have one without the other being affected."

In conclusion, Taylor's rise to stardom with her breakthrough album offers another valuable lesson in our exploration of 'Shake it Off – The Taylor Swift Way Of Standing Tall and Staying Real in a Shaky World - 34 Powerful Principles'. It shows us that success, fame, or recognition should not change who we are at our core. Taylor teaches us that authenticity resonates more powerfully than perfection. She shows us that it's more important to stay true to ourselves, tell our stories and, in the face of fame or criticism, to stand tall and stay real.

Chapter 8

Behind the Lyrics: The Songwriting Process Unveiled

Taylor Swift's songwriting prowess is as well-known as her singing abilities, a rare and incredible combination. Her lyrics have the power to transport listeners into her world, a journey into love, heartbreak, and resilience.

But how does Taylor conjure such intricate, relatable stories through her lyrics? How does she channel her emotions and experiences into songs that touch millions?

As fans would know, the art of storytelling has always been at the heart of Taylor's songwriting process. Taylor shared this sentiment in a 2019 interview with CBS Sunday Morning: "I want to write about emotions as they apply to me... every song I write is like a time capsule. It all comes from a place of truth."

The "place of truth" Taylor speaks of is where the magic begins. Taylor has an uncanny ability to take personal experiences, some blissful, others painful, and turn them into anthems. Songs like "Love Story," "Bad Blood," "We Are Never Ever Getting Back Together," are all born out of her personal life, making them resonate with fans who relate to similar situations.

While heartbreak is a common theme, Taylor doesn't shy away from tackling other subjects. Her song, "The Man," for instance, is a critique of double standards in society, showing her ability to interweave social commentary with catchy beats.

The next step in Taylor's songwriting process is the melody. She told NPR in 2014, "Melodies come to me very quickly. I'll have a strange melody pop into my head and think, 'What is this? It's interesting.'" It's this ear for unique melodies that add depth and texture to her lyrics.

Taylor's notebooks, filled with lyrics, doodles, and ideas, are famous. During a Tiny Desk concert in 2019, she mentioned her habit of writing ideas down, "I jot ideas down on my phone, in my notebook. Sometimes a phrase will inspire a whole song."

So, what can we learn from Taylor Swift's songwriting process?

First, it's all about authenticity. Being true to one's experiences and emotions makes art relatable, and it connects us to others who might feel the same.

Second, creativity is not always a lightning bolt of inspiration. It requires observation, curiosity, and patience, skills Taylor has honed over her career.

Lastly, don't be afraid to address real issues in your work. By tackling social issues like sexism, Taylor reminds us of the power of art to spark conversation and change.

In the spirit of our book title, 'Shake it Off – The Taylor Swift Way of Standing Tall and Staying Real in a Shaky World - 34 Powerful Principles,' Taylor's songwriting process reveals her commitment to staying real. It teaches us to embrace our experiences, to find our voice, and to use that voice to shake the world.

Even with her stunning success, Taylor's songwriting process remains remarkably humble. It's rooted in a curiosity about the world and people, a dedication to truth, and an unwavering belief in the power of stories. It's these qualities that allow her to consistently create music that resonates deeply with her fans.

For those seeking to apply Taylor's principles in their own lives, her songwriting journey imparts several valuable lessons. She teaches us the power of collaboration, the importance of continuous learning, and the courage to experiment and make mistakes. Her story also reinforces the value of staying true to your roots while being open to evolution and growth.

As we reflect on this chapter in Taylor Swift's life, it becomes clear that her songwriting process is not just about creating chart-topping hits – it's also about building connections, sharing experiences, and giving a voice to those who may struggle to articulate their feelings. Through her songs, Taylor gives us the courage to embrace our emotions, speak our truth, and above all, to stand tall and stay real in a shaky world.

Her philosophy could be summed up in her own words from the '1989' secret sessions in 2014, "I write songs to help you get past whatever you're stuck on, whether it's a relationship that ended badly, or just a frustrating situation. If a song I wrote can help you bounce back, then I did my job right."

Chapter 9

Love Story: The Romantic Influences in Taylor's Music

From the earliest days of her career, Taylor Swift has been known for her honest and deeply personal narratives about relationships. Even when she was a teenager releasing her debut album, Taylor was fearlessly open in exploring the many nuances of love, romance, and heartbreak in her music.

Her talent for capturing the delicate balance of euphoria and vulnerability in relationships has always been particularly striking. Taylor's song "Love Story," from her album 'Fearless,' is an excellent example of this. In the song, she beautifully reimagines the tragic tale of Romeo and Juliet with a more hopeful ending. Taylor has shared that this song was inspired by a love interest that her family and friends didn't approve of. But instead of feeling defeated, she wrote "Love Story" to rewrite her narrative. In an interview with Billboard in 2008, she explained, "I took that storyline and thought about what that would be like in modern times, and wrote a song about it."

Taylor's ability to draw from her own experiences for her music has been instrumental in helping fans worldwide relate to and find comfort in her songs. Her 2019 album 'Lover' is a testament to this, with songs like "Lover" and "Cornelia Street" presenting different dimensions of a love relationship. Yet, these songs aren't just tales of romance and love. They also contain powerful messages about growth, compromise, and mutual respect in relationships.

Despite the intense scrutiny her love life has received over the years, Taylor has remained steadfast in her approach to writing about her experiences. She has often emphasized that every individual has the right to express their feelings without being judged or criticized. Speaking to Elle magazine in 2019, Taylor said, "I've learned that just because someone is in your life for one part of your life, it doesn't mean they'll be in your life forever...That's okay. It's important to learn from those experiences."

From Taylor's perspective, love isn't just about romantic relationships. It also encompasses self-love and loving those around us. Her song "The Best Day," dedicated to her mother, and "Invisible String," an ode to the unseen ties that bind us, beautifully depict these broader concepts of love.

As we conclude this chapter, it's clear that Taylor's portrayal of love in her music isn't solely about romance. It's also about self-growth, empathy, and respect. These themes reinforce the 'Shake it Off' principles: standing tall in our experiences, staying real in our relationships, and understanding that every encounter teaches us something valuable. Remembering Taylor's own words from her '1989 World Tour' in 2015, "Every love story is important and worth telling. Each one teaches us something about ourselves."

Much of Taylor's music reveals a deep understanding of the human heart. From youthful crushes to tumultuous breakups, she has a gift for translating emotions into melodies that resonate with her fans. Beyond romantic love, her songs express a vast range of feelings, such as the unshakeable bonds of friendship in "Fifteen" and the strength of familial ties in "Never Grow Up."

Her fearless exploration of love in all its forms has earned her millions of fans worldwide, as well as a slew of awards. Taylor's knack for creating music that stirs the heart and soul lies in her ability to capture love's many layers. Every relationship, every story, is unique, and through her music, Taylor Swift acknowledges this diversity.

Chapter 10

Fans First: The Unique Bond Between Taylor and Her Fans

One of the many remarkable aspects of Taylor Swift's journey is her unique, heartfelt bond with her fans, often referred to as "Swifties." From the moment she stepped onto the music scene, Taylor's connection with her audience was different, deeper. She made it clear that her fans are not just a part of the journey, but the journey itself.

A warm, genuine and empathetic young woman, Taylor built her fanbase through authenticity, transparency, and kindness. Whether it's personally responding to fan letters or surprising them with secret sessions to debut her new albums, Taylor has consistently gone above and beyond to connect with her fans.

She's also been there for Swifties in their darkest hours. For instance, one fan had been homeless and pregnant, and Taylor helped her buy a home and set her life on track. Taylor's fan interactions aren't just meet-and-greeting; they're heartfelt connections. She has created a sense of community, love, and understanding around her music that fans deeply appreciate.

In an interview with Vanity Fair in 2015, she said, "I don't want to be just another many celebrities who show up to a photo shoot. I want to be somebody who has a deliberate, constant, and conscientious relationship with my fans."

Taylor's relationship with her fans hasn't always been smooth sailing. When her album 'Reputation' dropped, Taylor was embroiled in several public feuds. However, instead of letting the negativity cloud her bond with her fans, she embraced the controversy and used it as an opportunity for growth. She wrote and sang about her experiences, giving her fans a chance to understand her perspective and become a part of her journey.

This bond was tested again in the 'Scooter Braun' incident, where Taylor's early albums were sold without her permission. Instead of backing down, Swifties rallied around their icon, showing their support in every possible way. They stood by her side, just as she had stood by theirs.

She recognizes the impact of her words and actions on her fans. When she won the Album of the Year award for '1989' at the Grammy Awards 2016, she said, "I want to say to all the young women out there—there are going to be people along the way who will try to undercut your success...But if you just focus on the work and you don't let those people sidetrack you, someday when you get where you're going you'll look around and you will know that it was you and the people who love you who put you there. And that will be the greatest feeling in the world."

In this chapter, the 'Shake it Off' principle we can draw from Taylor's bond with her fans is that authentic connection is the foundation of true success. Through her respect and appreciation for her fans, Taylor shows us that standing tall and staying real isn't just about being true to ourselves, but also about being true to those who support and care for us.

Even in the face of adversity, Taylor has always stood by her fans. She treats them with the respect and love that they deserve, and in return, they give her unwavering support. This genuine and deep bond is a testament to Taylor's authenticity, and a shining example of how to stay real in a shaky world.

Swifties around the world cherish the personal touch that Taylor Swift adds to her fandom. She's made it a habit to reach out to her fans, reading letters, sending personalized gifts, and even inviting fans to her home for listening parties. These actions resonate deeply and foster a sense of closeness.

Let's take a look at the '1989 Secret Sessions' in 2014. Taylor invited fans to her various homes around the world, where they got to listen to her album '1989' before anyone else. She baked cookies, posed for pictures, and shared stories behind the songs. This wasn't just a promotional event; it was an expression of appreciation, an acknowledgement of the fans' unwavering support.

Chapter 11

Behind the Scenes: Unseen Moments from the World Tour

Imagine the thrill of stepping on stage, the bright lights hitting your face, and the deafening applause from thousands of adoring fans. The exhilaration of a Taylor Swift concert is a one-of-a-kind experience. But for Taylor herself, the journey doesn't start when she steps out into the limelight; it begins much earlier, behind the scenes.

Preparing for a world tour is a mammoth task. There are countless rehearsals, set designs to approve, costumes to fit, and soundchecks to attend. And yet, in the midst of it all, Taylor is known for her ability to create a fun and supportive atmosphere. She once revealed during an interview with 'Rolling Stone' in 2014, "I like to take the chaotic parts of my life and turn them into something I can control."

One of the favorite stories from Taylor's 'Speak Now World Tour' is about her tour family. Each person on the tour, from the dancers to the crew members, received a brightly colored, knitted scarf from Taylor during the holidays, a project she'd been secretly working on in her downtime. "We're not just a team, we're a family. And families take care of each other," she told 'BBC Radio 1' in 2011.

Taylor's tours aren't just about the music; they're about creating a sense of home and belonging, both for her fans and for her team. She once told a crowd during her '1989 World Tour', "You are not someone else's opinion of you. You are not damaged goods just because you've made mistakes in your life. You are a product of the lessons you've learned."

The tour, in many ways, is a reflection of Taylor herself. Despite the high-pressure environment, she always maintains a sense of grace, kindness, and inclusivity. She takes these values onto the stage, turning each performance into a celebration of individuality and resilience.

Summarizing this chapter, we've glimpsed behind the curtain of a Taylor Swift tour. We've discovered that for Taylor, it's about more than just singing songs and playing music. It's about building a community and creating an environment where everyone feels valued and loved.

"I love seeing these little bits of your lives happening in the crowd. It's like looking out at a sea of stars," she told 'Elle Magazine' in 2019. It is her habit to keep an eye out for heart-warming stories in the crowd, demonstrating how deeply she values her fans.

From this chapter, we can take away another powerful principle from the Taylor Swift way of standing tall and staying real: "Create a sense of belonging for those around you." This principle applies not only to professional relationships but to personal ones as well. Just as Taylor does, we can all strive to foster environments where people feel seen, appreciated, and free to be themselves.

The magic of a Taylor Swift concert is not only confined to her mesmerizing performances on stage, but also includes the intimate interactions with her fans. Taylor's genuine love for her supporters is one of the reasons her concerts feel more like a family gathering than a spectacle.

One such occasion was during the 'Reputation Stadium Tour' when Taylor spotted a fan's sign in the crowd that read, "I proposed to my girlfriend during Love Story!" Swift, moved by this romantic gesture, invited the couple backstage to congratulate them personally. This moment, as she revealed in an Instagram post, was one of her favorites from the tour.

Chapter 12

The Voices that Inspired: Taylor's Musical Influences

Before Taylor Swift became a household name, she was just a girl with big dreams and a guitar, finding inspiration in the artists whose music touched her heart. "I was influenced by all sorts of music," Taylor once mentioned in a 2010 interview with 'Time Magazine'. She stated that from pop to country to rock, all genres shaped her unique sound.

One of the most influential voices in her life was the country music legend, Shania Twain. In an interview with 'CMT Radio' in 2009, Swift shared, "Her music made me fall in love with country music. I think it was the way she was so bold and didn't care what anyone thought."

It wasn't just Shania's songs, but also her audacity and fearlessness that resonated with Taylor. Seeing another woman make music on her own terms, defying expectations, gave Taylor the courage to shake off the constraints and stay real in her own artistic journey.

Another pivotal influence was the Dixie Chicks. Their storytelling and emotional transparency struck a chord in Taylor's heart. In an interview with 'Billboard' in 2019, Taylor explained how their influence helped her in writing 'Soon You'll Get Better', a deeply personal track from her album 'Lover'.

"I listened to the Dixie Chicks' music a lot when I was a kid. Their ability to take an intensely personal experience and make it accessible to others is something I've always admired," she shared.

Swift also admired the rock world's legends like Bruce Springsteen and Tom Petty, as stated in a 2012 interview with 'Rolling Stone'. Their compelling storytelling and timeless songwriting were characteristics Taylor sought to emulate in her own work.

Every artist that inspired Taylor Swift shared a common thread - authenticity. They expressed their truths, undiluted and unfiltered, through their music. This trait deeply influenced Taylor's approach to her art.

Taylor Swift was also drawn to the honesty and vulnerability of singer-songwriters. Artists like Joni Mitchell, who wove personal narratives into their songs, resonated deeply with Taylor. "The way she wrote about her emotions was breathtaking to me," Taylor said about Joni Mitchell in a 2015 interview with the BBC Radio 1.

In conclusion, Taylor Swift's musical journey has been shaped by various artists, each imprinting a part of their style and philosophy on her. Her music, therefore, is a tapestry woven with threads borrowed from each of her influences. Yet, at the heart of it all, Taylor remains uniquely herself, standing tall in her authenticity and keeping it real in her lyricism.

From this chapter, we derive the principle: "Draw inspiration from those around you, but never lose sight of who you are." Let's apply this principle in our lives by embracing the wisdom and experiences of others, but never forgetting our essence in the process. It's through such balance that we can navigate the shaky world, just like Taylor Swift.

Taylor has often credited James Taylor as an instrumental influence in her music. In an interview with 'Entertainment Weekly' in 2011, Swift spoke about her admiration for James Taylor, stating, "I loved his voice, and his songwriting seemed very simple but was very profound and sort of reached into your heart and made you feel seen and understood."

James Taylor's music not only had a profound impact on Taylor's songwriting but also on her naming. Her parents named her after him in the hope she'd pursue a career in song-writing, as she revealed in a 2008 interview with 'The Telegraph'.

Perhaps the most modern of Swift's influences is the alt-rock band Paramore. In a conversation with 'Rolling Stone' in 2012, Swift revealed her appreciation for the band's lead singer Hayley Williams. "I love her unapologetic energy and her lyrics," she said. Williams' emotional intensity and honesty showed Swift that she could be bold in her music, too.

Chapter 13

Standing Tall: Overcoming Personal Obstacles

Success has not come without its challenges for Taylor Swift. The journey to stardom was often difficult, filled with both personal and professional obstacles that she had to navigate.

One of the most significant challenges Taylor faced early in her career was moving to Nashville at the young age of fourteen. Leaving behind her friends, her school, and everything familiar, Taylor took the leap and moved to a new city to pursue her dreams. The transition was challenging, but it was a risk she was willing to take. During a 2019 interview with CBS Sunday Morning, Taylor shared, "It was a really big risk for us, but it was a calculated one. We knew that this was the city where dreams come true, and I wanted to be a part of that."

Yet, the difficulties didn't stop there. In her pursuit of her dream, Taylor faced countless rejections from record labels. But instead of letting the rejections crush her spirit, she used them as fuel to work harder. Swift told 'People' magazine in 2010, "Every record label I tried to get into turned me down. I would play them a song on my guitar, and they would give me advice like 'come back when you're 18.' But I never let those rejections discourage me."

On a more personal note, Taylor has had to deal with scrutiny and criticism that comes with fame. Everything from her relationships to her songwriting has been under the public eye. But she's remained resilient. In a 2017 interview with 'Vogue', she stated, "There are going to be people along the way who will try to undercut your success or take credit for your accomplishments or your fame...But if you just focus on the work and you don't let those people sidetrack you, someday, you'll look around and you will know that it was you and the people who love you who put you there."

In recent years, Taylor has also faced significant personal challenges, including her mother's cancer diagnosis. But through it all, she's stayed strong, standing tall against these adversities. She's even used her music as an outlet for dealing with these difficult experiences, further demonstrating her incredible resilience.

To wrap up this chapter, the principle we learn from Taylor Swift's experiences is that the path to success is not always smooth. There will be obstacles and rejections along the way, but it's about how you overcome them. Swift teaches us that by standing tall in the face of adversity and staying true to ourselves, we can overcome any obstacle that comes our way. Her strength and resilience in overcoming these personal obstacles show us that it's not just about the destination, but the journey. And if we shake off the negativity and stay real to ourselves, we can thrive in even the shakiest of worlds.

In a world where tabloids and public scrutiny are often a harsh reality for celebrities, Taylor Swift's resilience is commendable. Even in the face of highly publicized legal battles, such as her stand against a DJ in 2017 who she claimed had assaulted her, Taylor stood tall. With grace and poise, she navigated this challenging period, later reflecting on the trial during her acceptance speech for TIME's Person of the Year in 2017. She said, "I figured that if he would be brazen enough to assault me under these risky circumstances and high stakes, imagine what he might do to a vulnerable, young artist if given the chance."

Chapter 14

Look Inside: Taylor's Personal Strengths Away from the Cameras

A megastar on stage, Taylor Swift's music and performances have touched millions of hearts worldwide. But what truly sets her apart are the personal strengths that she has nurtured and developed, far from the glare of the cameras.

One of the most striking of these strengths is her empathy. This extends beyond her close-knit circle of family and friends to her millions of fans. Her ability to understand and share the feelings of others shines through in her music, making it relatable to a wide range of listeners. Taylor's empathy is also apparent in her many philanthropic endeavors. She has consistently used her platform and resources to help those in need, from disaster relief efforts to educational initiatives.

In a 2012 interview with Katie Couric, Taylor revealed, "I think for me, it feels very natural to talk to teenagers and people my age... about feelings and what they're going through and their insecurities." This statement shows how her natural affinity for empathizing with others has fueled her songwriting and connection with fans.

Another personal strength is Taylor's resilience. In an industry known for its ups and downs, Taylor has proven time and again that she can bounce back from adversity. From disputes with fellow artists to navigating the complex world of music rights, she has shown an impressive ability to stand her ground.

During her acceptance speech at the 2016 Grammy Awards, Taylor said, "As the first woman to win Album of the Year at the Grammys twice, I want to say to all the young women out there: there are going to be people along the way who will try to undercut your success or take credit for your accomplishments or your fame... But if you just focus on the work and you don't let those people sidetrack you, someday when you get where you're going, you'll look around and you'll know that it was you and the people who love you who put you there, and that will be the greatest feeling in the world."

This quote not only exemplifies her resilience but also her independence and dedication to her craft. Taylor's career trajectory shows that while the road to success may not be smooth, determination and self-belief can help one overcome any hurdle.

Behind the glitz and glamour, it's Taylor's humility that keeps her grounded. Despite her meteoric rise to fame, she has remained surprisingly down-to-earth. Her fans and friends often praise her for this quality, which allows her to connect with people on a deeply human level.

As we wrap up this chapter, it's clear that Taylor's personal strengths away from the cameras are every bit as compelling as her public persona. Her empathy, resilience, and humility allow her to connect with people in a unique and profound way, serving as powerful reminders that it's not only talent, but also character that defines us.

Building further on the strengths of Taylor, one cannot overlook her integrity, both as an artist and a person. She believes in the authenticity of her words, her music, and her feelings, which shows in her unwavering commitment to writing her own songs. She once said in an interview with Time magazine in 2014, "There's a different vocabulary for men and women in the music industry. You need to just not be intimidated by that." It's this boldness to be true and authentic that makes Taylor a role model for many.

Another of Taylor's core strengths lies in her ability to adapt. In the music industry, relevance is everything, and staying on top means constantly evolving. From the country-inspired tones of her early albums to the pop anthems and indie vibes of her later works, Taylor has shown her versatility and readiness to take risks.

Chapter 15

Role Models: The Women Who Influenced Taylor Swift

As we've explored Taylor Swift's journey thus far, we've looked at her strengths, her struggles, and her unique relationships with music, fans, and love. It's crucial to understand that no one reaches where they are without some influence. Taylor Swift, an icon of resilience and authenticity, is no exception. In this chapter, let's unfold the stories of the women who have inspired Taylor and have helped shape her into the woman she stands as today.

First and foremost, we must begin with her mother, Andrea Swift. Andrea has been a pillar of strength and love for Taylor. In numerous interviews, Taylor has mentioned how her mother's unconditional love and support have shaped her. "She's always the first person I call when I have any sort of heartbreak or sadness, or you know, confusion," Swift revealed during an interview with CBS Sunday Morning in 2019. It's evident that Andrea's constant presence and support have been foundational in Taylor's personal and professional life.

In the world of music, one of Taylor's earliest inspirations was Shania Twain. Growing up, Taylor was captivated by Shania's bold, confident persona and the way she bent genres, blending country and pop in a way that hadn't been seen before. Swift told Rolling Stone in 2009, "She was just so strong. I thought it was incredibly brave of her to step out and do something different like that."

Another influential figure in Taylor's life has been the singer-songwriter Carly Simon. Known for her deeply personal style of songwriting, Carly has long been a model for Taylor's own lyricism. She famously joined Swift on stage during the Red Tour for a surprise duet, after which Swift confessed, "Before I bring out my special guest, I have this question that I've always, always had. I think a lot of you have probably had this question too, always wondered what the answer is. Who is this song 'You're So Vain' by Carly Simon written about?"

Last, but definitely not least, is her friend and fellow singer, Selena Gomez. Their friendship, dating back to their early teens, has been a source of constant support and inspiration. The way Gomez has handled her fame and personal struggles has deeply inspired Swift. During an interview with Zane Lowe on Apple Music's Beats 1 in 2019, Swift shared, "I knew from when I met her I would always have her back. In my life, I have the ability to forgive people who have hurt me. But I don't know if I can forgive someone who hurts her."

In conclusion, Taylor Swift's journey is intertwined with the strength, passion, and determination of the influential women in her life. From her mother's unwavering support to Shania Twain's genre-bending bravery, Carly Simon's lyrical profundity, and Selena Gomez's enduring friendship, Taylor has drawn from each of these remarkable women to stay tall and true to herself.

As we end this chapter, let us carry forward this powerful principle – our lives are shaped by those we allow to influence us. Let's choose our influences wisely and stand tall, shaking off the negatives while staying authentic in our journey, just like

Taylor Swift. An influential force in Taylor's journey as a woman and artist has undeniably been the women of country music. In the world of country music where Taylor's roots lie, legends like Dolly Parton and Faith Hill have made a lasting impact. Dolly's candidness about her life and her heartwarming, yet powerful, songs have been a beacon of inspiration. In a 2016 Vogue interview, Taylor shared, "Dolly Parton is such an amazing example to every female songwriter out there."

Chapter 16

Shaking Off the Haters: Navigating Fame and Criticism

Just like a coin has two sides, fame comes with its share of admiration and criticism. Taylor Swift has had an impressive career, but it has not been without its challenges. Swift has faced criticism on many fronts, from her songwriting to her personal life, but she has always found a way to navigate through the sea of criticism with grace and resilience.

One of the criticisms often aimed at Swift is her songwriting, with some arguing that she only writes about her breakups. To this, Taylor has always maintained a steadfast position: she writes about her life, and if that includes heartbreak, then so be it. As she said in an interview with Vanity Fair in 2013, "For a female to write about her feelings, and then be portrayed as some clingy, insane, desperate girlfriend in need of making you marry her and have kids with her, I think that's taking something that potentially should be celebrated—a woman writing about her feelings in a confessional way—and twisting it into something that is frankly a little sexist."

Another aspect of criticism Taylor has faced is about her relationships. People have often made speculations and assumptions about her dating life. But Taylor has always been straightforward about her perspective. In a radio interview with NPR in 2014, Taylor shared, "The most important thing for me is maintaining artistic integrity, which means as a songwriter I still continue to write about my life."

Taylor also faced a storm of backlash during her feud with Kanye West and Kim Kardashian in 2016. However, instead of succumbing to the negativity, she turned it into an opportunity for growth and used it as a fuel for her album "Reputation". In her Netflix documentary, "Miss Americana," Swift talks about how she coped with the incident, stating, "I realized I had to restructure my life because it felt completely out of control."

What stands out in all these instances is Taylor's ability to 'shake it off' and stay true to herself, no matter how intense the criticism. She turns her experiences into songs, sharing her truths with her fans, and this is one of the many reasons why her fans admire her so much.

Despite the challenges and criticisms, Taylor Swift has always found ways to use these instances as a source of strength and inspiration for her music. Her reaction to criticism and public scrutiny embodies the principle of turning negatives into positives. She once stated during her concert in 2018, "You don't have to feel like a wasted space. You're original, cannot be replaced."

Her ability to channel negative experiences into creativity is a key aspect of her resilience. For instance, after a public breakup, she channeled her feelings into the song "Back to December," turning a personal hardship into a universal anthem of regret and longing. As Taylor once said in an interview with Glamour in 2014, "Every one of my regrets has produced a song I'm proud of."

In conclusion, the key takeaway from this chapter is that criticism is inevitable, especially when you are in the public eye. But how you respond to it is what truly matters. Taylor Swift stands as a testament to the fact that you can rise above the negativity, continue doing what you love, and remain authentic to who you are. This is the "Taylor Swift way of standing tall and staying real in a shaky world". And as we continue this journey, let's remember that we too can 'shake it off' and focus on our own path.

Chapter 17

The Ladder of Success: Taylor's Perseverance in her Career

The world sees Taylor Swift as an accomplished star, but the journey towards the pinnacle of success was steeped in dedication and perseverance. Taylor Swift's journey shows us that success isn't about luck; it's about perseverance, passion, and commitment to one's craft.

Taylor moved to Nashville at the young age of 14 to pursue her dreams, showing an incredible determination that was far beyond her years. She had her first recording deal fall through, a setback that might have discouraged many. But in the words of Taylor herself, during a speech at the Grammy Museum in 2015, she said, "I think when you're a little kid, you're fearless. You're not yet conditioned to be afraid of failing."

Taylor's commitment to her music is beyond just writing and performing. She plays a key role in the production of her albums, ensuring her music remains authentic and true to her vision. In her documentary "Miss Americana" (2020), she said, "I want to make music and perform for the rest of my life, it's all I've ever known."

Swift's career has also seen public disputes, such as her fight for artist's rights against music industry moguls. She has stood her ground, showing immense courage and perseverance. In an op-ed for the Wall Street Journal in 2014, she wrote, "In the future, artists will get record deals because they have fans—not the other way around."

Her determination to take control of her music was further exemplified when she decided to re-record her old albums, a move that was unheard of. This decision was a testament to her resilience and determination to keep her music truly hers.

As we wrap up this chapter, we take away a valuable principle from Taylor Swift's journey: Perseverance is the key to achieving success. Despite setbacks and challenges, Taylor Swift stayed committed to her dreams, demonstrating that it's not the hurdles that define us, but how we overcome them.

In Taylor's words during her concert in Columbus, 2018, she said, "You are not going backward, you are just changing", a testament to the importance of persistence and adaptability in the journey towards success. Taylor Swift's journey teaches us to stand tall, to persistently pursue our dreams, and stay real to our values even in the shaky world of the music industry. This is the Taylor Swift way – standing tall and staying real.

Taylor was just a teenager when she entered the music industry, an industry known for its ruthlessness. In her 2019 MTV VMA acceptance speech for the 'Video of the Year' award, she said, "You voting for this video means that you want a world where we're all treated equally under the law". This comment illustrates her maturity and the sense of responsibility she felt, not just towards her career but also towards her fans and society at large.

The intense scrutiny and pressure that came with her increasing fame were monumental. Every move she made, every word she spoke, was under the public eye. She was expected to be perfect, to fit into the mould that society had for her. However, Taylor chose to defy these expectations. Instead, she remained true to herself, refusing to lose her authenticity. Her lyrics often reflected these challenges. In her song, "The Lucky One" (2012), she sings, "And they tell you that you're lucky, but you're so confused cause you don't feel pretty, you just feel used." It showcased the struggles of being in the limelight.

Despite all these obstacles, Taylor persisted, demonstrating not just her passion for music but also her strength and courage. It's an important lesson for all Swifties and aspiring musicians out there – it's essential to keep striving for your dreams, no matter the difficulties that come your way. It's this relentless determination that has solidified Taylor's position as one of the most influential artists of our generation.

Wrapping up this chapter, we've learned from Taylor Swift that success isn't always about the applause and the awards. It's about being true to oneself, staying grounded in your values, and persisting through the ups and downs. It's about learning to 'shake it off' and standing tall through the challenges. And that, dear readers, is the 'Taylor Swift way' – the path of resilience, authenticity, and unwavering determination.

Chapter 18

Her Shaky World: Dealing with Public Life and Maintaining Privacy

With her meteoric rise to fame, Taylor Swift's world quickly became a shaky one. Every aspect of her life was suddenly under the microscope, leading to a constant struggle for privacy. Yet, despite the storm that often swirled around her, Taylor found ways to maintain her calm, her authenticity, and most importantly, her sanity.

Taylor's life is a paradox of extreme public attention and a relentless fight for privacy. In the midst of the flashing lights and constant public scrutiny, she learnt to carve out private moments for herself, away from the public eye. Her resilience in dealing with these challenges is an inspiration to many.

In an interview with Billboard in 2019, Taylor remarked, "You have to make a decision, early on, about how much you want to let into your world." These profound words give us a glimpse into her approach towards privacy in a world where her every move is under scrutiny.

A striking example of her fight for privacy was during her '1989' era when she was rarely seen in public. She used disguises, traveled at odd hours, and even walked backward to avoid the paparazzi! While some may find it amusing, it is a testament to the lengths she would go to maintain her sanity in a world that constantly wanted more of her.

Her approach to social media is another testament to her desire for privacy. Taylor uses social media to connect with her fans, share her music and provide snippets of her life. But she is mindful of not letting it cross into her private space. She believes in sharing moments that matter, rather than creating moments for sharing.

Yet, amidst all this, Taylor has never lost her connection with her fans. She frequently interacts with them on social media, and her secret sessions are now legendary, where she invites fans to her home to listen to her new album before it's released. Her love for her fans is evident in these interactions - she shares her world with them while still retaining her much-needed private space.

So, how does Taylor 'shake it off' and stand tall amidst this shaky world of fame and constant public scrutiny? It comes down to her ability to draw boundaries, to decide what she lets into her world, and her steadfast commitment to maintain her privacy.

In conclusion, this chapter has shown us that even amidst the shaky world of fame and constant public scrutiny, it's crucial to draw boundaries and protect one's privacy. Taylor Swift has shown us that it is possible to be a global superstar yet still maintain a private life. The 'Taylor Swift way' isn't just about standing tall; it's about standing tall with dignity, authenticity, and respect for oneself.

In her public life, Taylor Swift has faced endless controversies and critiques, which have not only challenged her professionally but personally as well. In the midst of this shaky world, she has demonstrated an extraordinary strength and a remarkable knack for dealing with these pressures.

One of Taylor's most inspiring attributes is her ability to use the criticisms and controversies as fuel for her art. A testament to this is her award-winning album, 'Reputation'. Following a series of personal and public controversies, Taylor used the critique as a catalyst, transforming her experiences into music. She once shared in a Vogue interview in 2019, "When they stop you from doing something, when they stop you from rising, just create something else."

Chapter 19

Resilience in the Public Eye: Handling Media and Controversy

Few people understand the pressure of living in the public eye more than Taylor Swift. From her rise to stardom at a young age, she has had to navigate a world that has been both enchanted by her talent and ever ready to scrutinize her every move. It's within this intense, sometimes turbulent world that Taylor has shown resilience and grace.

During her 2009 MTV Video Music Awards acceptance speech, an unexpected interruption occurred that would stir controversy. Kanye West, another renowned artist, took to the stage and belittled her achievement in front of a worldwide audience. This incident would have left many feeling defeated, but not Taylor. She turned that painful event into a learning experience, and in her 2010 song "Innocent", she extended an olive branch, teaching her fans the power of forgiveness.

Taylor once said during a concert in Tokyo in 2014, "You are not the opinion of somebody who doesn't know you. You are not damaged goods just because you've made mistakes in your life. You are not going nowhere just because you haven't gotten where you want to go yet."

Throughout her career, Taylor has been at the center of several controversies and misunderstandings, often misrepresented by tabloids. However, instead of retreating, Taylor learned to speak her truth, most notably in her 2019 blog post where she openly addressed her struggle to retain ownership of her music. This honesty not only gave her fans a glimpse of the real challenges she faced but also served as a beacon of hope for other artists.

Taylor Swift's ability to handle media scrutiny and controversy exemplifies her resilience. Her approach is not about denying the existence of these challenges, but rather about acknowledging them, learning from them, and using them to fuel her journey forward.

She once told 'Elle' magazine in 2019, "I've learned that you can't let your worth be defined by what people say about you in the media. Your value doesn't decrease based on someone's inability to see your worth."

Taylor's resilience doesn't mean she's immune to the pressures of her fame, but rather, she's learned to cope with them in her own unique way. In her documentary, "Miss Americana," she opened up about her struggles with eating disorders, body image issues, and the intense loneliness that fame often brings.

To conclude this chapter, Taylor Swift's resilience in the face of media scrutiny and controversy stands as a powerful lesson. It teaches us that we have the power to define ourselves, irrespective of the noise and negativity in our environment. Taylor's journey shows us that when the world feels shaky, we can, just like Taylor, "shake it off", stand tall, and stay real. It's about transforming challenges into opportunities and staying true to oneself. In essence, this is the Taylor Swift Way.

Despite these trying times, Taylor never lost sight of who she truly is. She demonstrated an uncanny knack for using controversy as a catalyst for her personal and creative growth. One notable incident was the criticism she received for her perceived lack of political engagement during the 2016 United States Presidential Election. Rather than ignoring the criticism, Taylor took it to heart. In a major turn in her career, she broke her political silence and used her platform to endorse candidates and express her political views during the 2018 mid-term elections.

Chapter 20

Standing Tall: Taylor's Journey towards Empowerment

Taylor Swift has always been an emblem of empowerment. She began her career as a young, enthusiastic girl with big dreams, and it was her steadfast commitment to those dreams that launched her into superstardom. Today, Taylor stands tall as one of the most influential women in the music industry, and her journey towards empowerment is an inspiring narrative filled with courage, resilience, and authenticity.

One of Taylor's most defining moments of empowerment came during a turbulent time in her career – the dispute with her former record label, Big Machine Label Group, over the ownership of her music catalog. In a public Tumblr post in 2019, she expressed her heartache, "For years I asked, pleaded for a chance to own my work. Instead, I was given an opportunity to sign back up to Big Machine Records and 'earn' one album back at a time, one for every new one I turned in. I walked away because I knew once I signed that contract, Scott Borchetta would sell the label, thereby selling me and my future."

Not one to back down, Taylor took a powerful stand and announced she would be re-recording her entire catalog, a decision that not only asserted her control over her music but also set an example for other artists in similar situations. On Good Morning America in 2019, she made her stand clear, "It's something that I'm very excited about doing because my contract says that starting November 2020, I can record albums 1 through 5 all over again. I'm very excited about it. I think artists deserve to own their work. I just feel very passionately about that."

Taylor's journey towards empowerment goes beyond her professional life. She has been a strong advocate for victims of sexual harassment, and her victory in the courtroom in 2017 against a radio DJ who had harassed her was another testament to her strength. "I'm not going to let you or your client make me feel in any way that this is my fault," she said during the trial, standing her ground. This moment was more than just a personal victory for Taylor – it was a statement for women everywhere, reinforcing the idea that it's essential to stand up against injustice, no matter how powerful the adversary might seem.

Taylor Swift's journey of empowerment reminds us that standing tall doesn't always mean being on top. Sometimes, it means standing up for what's right, fighting for what we believe in, and above all, staying true to ourselves. As we conclude this chapter, remember this vital principle from Taylor's journey: Real empowerment comes from owning your story, standing your ground, and refusing to be silenced. As Taylor once said, "There will be people along the way who will try to undercut your success... But if you just focus on the work and you don't let those people sidetrack you, someday, you'll look around and you will know that it was you and the people who love you who put you there. And that will be the greatest feeling in the world." So, 'shake it off' and keep moving forward, for the world is yours to conquer.

Beyond her direct influence on fans, Taylor has also played a significant role in pushing for change within the music industry. Her bold move to leave her record label in pursuit of creative and financial freedom, her advocacy for fair pay for artists on streaming platforms, and her determination to re-record her music all stand testament to her willingness to shake the status quo for the better.

In the face of adversity, Taylor Swift's response has consistently been to stand tall and fight for what she believes in. She shakes off criticism and uses her experiences as a means to empower herself and others.

As we conclude Chapter 20, remember the powerful principle evident in Taylor's journey: Empowerment isn't just about standing up for yourself. It's also about using your influence to make a positive impact on others and the world around you. As Taylor aptly puts it, "No matter what happens in life, be good to people. Being good to people is a wonderful legacy to leave behind." As you navigate your own shaky world, keep this principle in mind. Stand tall, shake it off, and remember the power you hold.

Chapter 21

Activism and Advocacy: Taylor's Efforts Off the Stage

Taylor's life, it's essential to acknowledge her role not just as an artist, but also as an activist and advocate. With the same vigor she brings to her music, Taylor Swift has committed to using her influence to shape the world positively.

One aspect of Taylor's activism that stands out is her dedication to LGBTQ+ rights. "Rights are being stripped from basically everyone who isn't a straight white cisgender male," she told Vogue in an interview in 2019. This awareness has seen her consistently express support for the community, notably with her single "You Need to Calm Down," which addresses homophobia. She also made a generous donation to the Tennessee Equality Project, pushing for LGBTQ+ rights in her home state.

However, it doesn't stop there. Taylor has been a strong advocate for artists' rights within the music industry. In her open letter to Apple Music in 2015, she voiced the importance of fair pay for artists, leading to the tech giant altering its payment policy for artists during the trial period of its streaming service.

But perhaps the most personal to Taylor has been her fight for ownership of her music. After a high-profile dispute with her former record label, she took a bold step to reclaim her work by re-recording her albums. This move not only highlighted the importance of artists' rights over their creations but also inspired other artists to consider their contracts more carefully.

Taylor's philanthropic work is also worth noting. Over the years, she has donated to numerous causes, including disaster relief, education, and cancer research. In 2012, she donated $4 million to the Country Music Hall of Fame to fund the Taylor Swift Education Center.

Off the stage, Taylor's advocacy work, a lesser-known facet of her life, also took flight. Her impassioned letters to politicians and statements on social media sparked a wave of public discourse. In an interview for Elle Magazine in 2019, she confessed, "I took a lot of time educating myself on the political system and the branches of government that are signing off on bills that affect our day-to-day life. I saw so many issues that put our most vulnerable citizens at risk, and felt like I had to speak up to try and help make a change."

One of Taylor's most impactful moments was her open letter to Apple in 2015. Unhappy with the company's initial decision not to pay artists during Apple Music's trial period, she penned a well-crafted letter that led to a policy reversal. It wasn't just a win for her, but for smaller artists struggling to make ends meet. Her action highlighted the principle that we should always stand up for what is right, even if it means confronting influential forces.

Furthermore, Taylor's advocacy for LGBTQ+ rights has been consistently inspiring. In 2019, she released the music video for "You Need to Calm Down," featuring numerous LGBTQ+ celebrities and ending with a petition for the Senate to pass the Equality Act. During a live performance on Good Morning

America the same year, she declared, "Equality is something that we all deserve."

In conclusion, Taylor Swift's activism and advocacy off the stage. It is yet another testament to her character, showing how she uses her voice not just in her music, but to speak up for those who often can't. The principle we draw from this chapter is the courage to use one's platform, regardless of its size, to advocate for what one believes in. Taylor Swift truly personifies this principle, proving that she is not just an artist, but a social advocate.

"I believe in the fight for LGBTQ+ rights, and that any form of discrimination based on sexual orientation or gender is WRONG," Taylor wrote on her Instagram during Pride Month in 2019. This commitment to advocacy shows how she stands tall in the face of adversity and stays real to her values, thereby shaking off any negativity that the world might bring. This chapter teaches us that we can all do the same in our lives, championing the causes we believe in, and thereby leaving a lasting impact on the world.

Chapter 22

Shaking Off the Pressure: Mental Health in the Limelight

Taylor Swift, despite her life in the glaring spotlight, has not been immune to the pressures and emotional struggles that accompany fame. The limelight, often thought of as glamorous, carries a weight that can lead to mental health challenges. Taylor has navigated this with grace and openness, inspiring millions with her journey.

At the 2019 TIME 100 Gala, Taylor shared a quote that rings with truth: "I've learned that you have to balance things out in your life. You can't have performance high without the jitters and fear." These words provide a glimpse into Taylor's understanding of the balance between personal wellbeing and professional pressures.

In her Netflix documentary "Miss Americana," Taylor opened up about her struggles with an eating disorder. The pressure to fit into the perfect image projected by the media and the industry had pushed her into an unhealthy relationship with food. Speaking about it, she shared that she had to learn to stop hating every ounce of fat on her body. This revelation was powerful and resonated with fans globally, highlighting the significance of mental health, body positivity, and self-love.

She also touched on the isolation and loneliness that fame can often bring. Despite being surrounded by people, the feeling of being alone and misunderstood was profound. "A lot of the time, I need to vent about stuff, and people just want to hear the happy things," she shared in an interview with CBS Sunday Morning in 2019. This openness about her struggles underscores her authenticity and helps fans understand the importance of acknowledging and discussing mental health.

Taylor's handling of her anxiety is another area where she leads by example. She has often spoken about the anxiety caused by her career, which she manages through her love for songwriting. Turning pressure into productivity, she told Elle in 2019, "I've learned that my anxiety has triggers and that I can minimize them."

To wrap up, Chapter 22 unveils Taylor's battle with mental health in the limelight. She teaches us the importance of acknowledging our struggles, seeking help when needed, and transforming pressure into productivity. This principle aligns perfectly with our book's theme, reminding us that even in a shaky world, we can shake off the pressure and stand tall. We delve into how Taylor Swift uses her platform to raise awareness about mental health. She acknowledges the influence she has on her fans and understands that by sharing her struggles, she can help others who may be facing similar difficulties.

In an interview with Vogue in 2019, Taylor spoke of the pressure of being a role model, stating, "It's not about perfection. It's about continuing to make better decisions." Here, Taylor subtly emphasizes the power of self-improvement, understanding that everyone, including herself, is human, with their unique struggles and mistakes.

Taylor also uses her songwriting as a means of expressing and coping with her mental health. She's written numerous songs that fans have related to their struggles, notably "The Archer" and "Clean." Her words have a soothing effect, reassuring fans that it's okay to experience anxiety and stress and that they're not alone.

She's also demonstrated the importance of self-care in managing mental health. In a 2019 interview with Elle, Taylor shared her self-care routine, "I make countdowns for things I'm excited about. I've learned that happiness is something we have to practice every day." Through her words, she taught us to cherish and look forward to the little things in life.

Chapter 23

Never Back Down: Taylor's Steadfast Approach to Life

As we delve into Chapter 23, we examine a unique characteristic that sets Taylor Swift apart — her steadfastness. Being steady and unwavering in the face of challenges is not something everyone can do, but Taylor shows us how to embrace this quality and use it as a pillar of strength.

Taylor Swift, like anyone else, has had her fair share of ups and downs. However, her resilience in the face of adversity has always been remarkable. This tenacity is evident in her personal life, her career, and her advocacy work.

Remember the time Taylor Swift stood her ground in her legal battle against a radio DJ in 2017? She was strong and assertive, taking a stand for herself and others who may have experienced similar situations. She was quoted saying, "I'm not going to let you or your client make me feel in any way that this is my fault because it isn't." This statement, made in court, echoed around the world, inspiring millions to never back down in the face of injustice.

Her perseverance is also clear in her music career. When she decided to transition from country to pop music with her album "1989," she faced skepticism and criticism. Still, she persisted, believing in her creative vision. This album went on to be a massive success, proving that taking risks can lead to great rewards.

Taylor has also displayed unwavering commitment to her beliefs and causes she supports. During the 2018 American Music Awards, she made a powerful statement encouraging her fans to vote. "This award and every single award given out tonight were voted on by the people, and you know what else is voted on by the people?" she said, "the midterm elections on November 6. Get out and vote."

Her steadfastness also reverberates in the way she treats her fans. Taylor never steps back when it comes to appreciating and interacting with her fanbase. Despite her monumental fame, she's held several "Secret Sessions" where she invites fans to her home to listen to her upcoming albums. This commitment shows how much she values her fans, always eager to connect with them on a personal level.

One quote from Taylor Swift that seems fitting to this context came from an interview with Vanity Fair in 2013, where she said, "In my mind, I'm still 15-years-old, from a small town, and I'm just astonished by all of this." It encapsulates her humility and groundedness, which is undoubtedly a contributing factor to her unwavering stance in life.

In conclusion, Chapter 23 shows us that standing tall even in the shakiest of circumstances is one of Taylor Swift's key principles. She never backs down, whether it's her creative choices, legal battles, or advocating for what she believes in. It's a powerful lesson for all of us, a testament to the strength we can all tap into when we decide not to back down.

It's not just about her career or standing up for herself, but it's also about her relationships. Even amidst a whirlwind of public scrutiny and media intrusion, Taylor has consistently held firm to her values, making it clear that she won't let external pressures define her personal life.

This principle was beautifully illustrated in her song "Lover," where she candidly shared the matured version of love she now understands, showing us that even in the shaky realm of romance, she remains firm, authentic, and genuine.

Chapter 24

Authenticity: Being True to Herself in the Midst of Fame

Authenticity, at its core, is about staying true to who you are, your values, and your beliefs. No matter what life throws at you. In this chapter, we turn our focus to a trait that is at the heart of Taylor Swift's identity — her authentic self. Taylor has shown the world that no matter how bright the lights, no matter how loud the applause, she will always be herself.

Being authentic in the public eye is not always an easy task, especially in an industry that often requires you to put on a mask. Despite this, Taylor has been nothing but true to herself throughout her career. Her authenticity is one of the reasons her fans adore her. They can relate to her experiences because they're real, they're human, and they're unapologetically Taylor.

Consider her journey in the music industry. Taylor began her career as a country singer. But as she grew and evolved, so did her music. She didn't stick to country music because it was expected or because it was safe. She experimented, pushed boundaries, and ended up dominating the pop music world with her album, "1989". This daring move was an act of authenticity— an expression of her evolving musical interests.

As Taylor once said during an interview with Barbara Walters in 2014, "If you're lucky enough to be different, don't ever change." These words reflect her approach to life, her career, and her personal identity.

Another testament to Taylor's authenticity is how she has handled her relationships in the public eye. Despite intense media scrutiny, she has always remained open about her experiences, sharing her feelings through her music. Tracks like "Back to December" and "Out of The Woods" serve as heartfelt apologies and confessions, reminding us all that even superstars have regrets and make mistakes.

Perhaps the most telling example of Taylor's authenticity comes from her own struggles with self-image. Like many young women, Taylor struggled with her body image, a topic she openly discussed in her Netflix documentary, "Miss Americana." By sharing her personal struggles, she let down her guard and allowed the world to see her vulnerabilities. She said, "I think a lot of us have a goal, and we're really disciplined, and that can lead us down a path that isn't necessarily healthy."

One of the unique ways Taylor Swift manifests her authenticity is through her songwriting. Her lyrics are personal and evocative, often telling stories directly from her life. The song "All Too Well," from her red album, is a perfect example. Taylor explained to Pop Dust in 2012 that it was "the hardest to write on the album because it took me a long time to filter through everything I wanted to say. It started out as a 10-minute song, which you can't put on an album."

Her ability to turn personal experiences into universal narratives allows her fans to see parts of their own lives reflected in her music. This only further cements the connection between Taylor and her fans, a bond that is genuinely rooted in authenticity and understanding

In conclusion, Taylor Swift's authenticity is one of her most powerful traits. It is her unwavering commitment to staying true to herself, regardless of fame or public opinion, that makes her a true role model. By embracing her unique path and expressing her feelings openly, she inspires us to do the same. Taylor teaches us that being authentic is not about being perfect or pleasing everyone. Instead, it's about being true to ourselves and our values, even in a shaky world.

Chapter 24 has taught us the importance of remaining authentic, no matter what. It is this authenticity that shines brightly in Taylor Swift's career and personal life, shaping her into the person she is today. From her music to her struggles and her approach to relationships, Taylor has shown that the road to success is paved with authenticity. It's a powerful lesson for us all to embrace our own paths, even in the face of adversity, and to never stray from who we truly are.

Chapter 25

Reputation and Redemption: Rising from the Ashes

Every story has its highs and lows, and Taylor Swift's journey is no exception. In this chapter, we will journey through Taylor's reputation era, a time marked by media backlash, personal turmoil, and ultimate redemption.

In 2016, Taylor's public image suffered a significant blow. A disagreement with Kanye West and Kim Kardashian, coupled with her high-profile breakup with Calvin Harris, turned public sentiment against her. Taylor's previously immaculate image was tarnished, and she became a subject of mockery on social media. The incident forced Taylor to step away from the limelight, but it also set the stage for one of her most potent creative periods.

Swift described this challenging time during her acceptance speech at the Billboard Women in Music event in 2019, saying, "I realized I had a choice to make: you can let it destroy you, or you can use it as fuel to power your next steps."

She chose the latter, and in 2017, she released her sixth studio album titled "Reputation." This album was Taylor's response to the negativity and backlash she received. It was more than just an album; it was a statement. Songs like "Look What You Made Me Do" and "I Did Something Bad" showed a darker, fiercer Taylor, one unafraid to stand her ground.

But her music also revealed her vulnerability. In songs like "Delicate" and "New Year's Day," we saw a Taylor Swift who wasn't invincible but was certainly resilient. It was a side of Taylor that many hadn't seen before, a human side that many could relate to.

The success of "Reputation" marked her triumphant return to music. Despite the controversies, the album debuted at number one on the Billboard 200 and received a positive reception from fans and critics alike. The subsequent "Reputation Stadium Tour" was a record-breaking success and served as a testament to Taylor's enduring appeal.

Perhaps the most poignant moment of her redemption arc was her performance of "Long Live" at the Reputation Tour, a song originally from her "Speak Now" album. While singing the lyrics "Long live all the mountains we moved, I had the time of my life fighting dragons with you," tears welled up in her eyes. It was a moment that seemed to say, "I've made it through, and I'm stronger because of it."

While the initial response to her tumultuous times was the powerful and edgy "Reputation," Taylor's journey of redemption continued on her following album, "Lover." Released in 2019, this album represented a transition from the darker themes of "Reputation" to more uplifting, love-centered tunes. Taylor Swift was back in her element, exuding authenticity, happiness, and creative brilliance.

"Lover" was a reflection of a new Taylor Swift, a woman who had braved the storm, faced her fears, and emerged stronger. The album allowed fans to celebrate her redemption and shared in her joy and growth. It was a reaffirmation that no setback is too great to overcome, and redemption is always within reach.

To wrap up this chapter, Taylor Swift's story during the "Reputation" era shows us that even the most challenging times can lead to powerful transformations. This era was a testament to Taylor's resilience, her ability to create, to heal, and to rise again. It also reminded us that every reputation has more than one side, and each of us has the power to redefine ours.

In Taylor's own words during her 2019 VMA's acceptance speech, "You voting for this video means that you want a world where we're all treated equally under the law, regardless of who we love, regardless of how we identify... I want to thank you for that. You are the reason why I have the opportunity to stand on this stage and do what I love doing." In every setback lies the seed of a comeback. Taylor Swift shook off the ashes, standing taller, stronger, and more genuine than ever before, showing us all the Taylor Swift way of resilience and redemption.

Chapter 26

The Strength to Carry On: Dealing with Loss and Heartbreak

As we journey further into Taylor Swift's life, we encounter another aspect of her strength — the power to persist despite the sting of loss and heartbreak. In Chapter 26, we explore how Taylor used these challenging experiences as a catalyst for personal growth and creative expression.

Taylor Swift's music has often been a canvas on which she paints her heartbreaks. She has never shied away from pouring her emotions into her lyrics, offering solace to those under-going similar experiences. It's almost like she has been using her music as a form of therapy, not only for herself but also for her listeners.

Take her album "Red," for instance. A deeply personal album, it became a powerful anthology of heartbreak, loss, and even-tual healing. The song "All Too Well," which Swift once described as the hardest to write on the album, is known for its detailed and emotive storytelling. It illustrates the profound impact heartbreak can have and the struggle to move forward.

Heartbreak, however, isn't only about romantic relationships. For Taylor, it also extends to losing friendships and facing betrayals, as reflected in songs like "Bad Blood." She has expressed the pain of losing a friend in a feud through this song, showing her fans that heartbreak isn't exclusive to romantic entanglements.

As the famous saying goes, "In the middle of difficulty lies opportunity." Taylor indeed found opportunities amid heartbreak. In an interview with ELLE magazine in 2019, Taylor mentioned, "I learned that disarming someone's petty bullying can be as simple as learning to laugh. In my experience, I've come to see that bullies want to be feared and taken seriously."

Even amidst loss, Taylor found strength. In 2020, her mother, Andrea Swift, was diagnosed with a brain tumor, a devastating blow to the Swift family. This personal loss heavily influenced her album "Evermore," particularly the song "Marjorie," a tribute to her late grandmother.

Her 2012 album, "Red," was particularly emblematic of this phase. "I call it my 'All Too Well' album," she said in an interview with Rolling Stone. "The album I wrote right after a big heartbreak, and it might be the only match for this one in terms of its impact on my life." This quote is an acknowledgment of her strength to carry on and turn her experiences into art.

One poignant story that stands out is the loss of her close friend, Cory Monteith, in 2013. Taylor had dedicated her song "Ronan" to him, highlighting how the impact of loss is far-reaching and deep. It showed her ability to empathize with others' pain, channel it into her work, and provide comfort for those who have experienced similar losses.

Taylor also faced loss when her catalogue was bought by Scooter Braun in 2019, an incident that deeply upset her. She wrote a heartfelt Tumblr post sharing her feelings, "This is my worst-case scenario. This is what happens when you sign a deal at fifteen to someone for whom the term 'loyalty' is clearly just a contractual concept."

However, she managed to turn this situation around, standing tall in the face of adversity. She decided to re-record her old albums, an ongoing effort that's been received enthusiastically by her fans worldwide. The process has allowed her to regain control over her music and has served as a powerful symbol of her resilience.

In conclusion, Chapter 26 delves into Taylor's strength in facing loss and heartbreak. She teaches us to remain true to our emotions, channel them productively, and find strength within ourselves to carry on. She demonstrates how to stand tall and stay real, even when the world seems to crumble around us.

This chapter in Taylor's life teaches us that it's okay to experience heartbreak and loss. It doesn't define us, but rather, it's what we do in the face of these experiences that truly shapes our character. As Taylor Swift once said, "No matter what happens in life, be good to people. Being good to people is a wonderful legacy to leave behind."

Chapter 27

Swift's Legacy: Her Impact on Young Artists

The influence of Taylor Swift extends far beyond her incredible discography and global fan base. Her impact on young artists, in particular, has been substantial and continues to shape the music industry.

Taylor Swift is not just an artist; she is a mentor, a beacon of hope, and a role model for many aspiring singers and songwriters. Her journey, her triumphs, her struggles, and her tenacity provide valuable lessons to young artists carving their own paths in music.

One key aspect of Taylor's influence is her genuine commitment to her craft. She has always been a storyteller, taking snippets of her life and weaving them into memorable songs. When asked about her writing process in a 2019 interview with Rolling Stone, she said, "I want to write songs that feel like they were written by a 30-year-old woman, not the girl who wrote 'Love Story.' I want my lyrics to grow up with me." This dedication to authentic self-expression is a beacon for young artists.

Swift's fight for artists' rights is another facet of her impact. Her public battles for fair compensation from streaming services, and control over her master recordings, have high-lighted significant issues within the music industry. In her open letter to Apple Music, she wrote, "We don't ask you for free iPhones. Please don't ask us to provide you with our music for no compensation." This has inspired many young artists to understand the importance of advocating for themselves.

Taylor's openness about her struggles and victories, both personal and professional, has given young artists a real-world look at what it means to navigate the music industry. She's shown that it's okay to stand up for yourself, to be true to who you are, and to let your experiences, good or bad, inspire your art.

One of the many young artists Taylor has influenced is Billie Eilish, who once said, "Taylor's music is proof that pop songs should make you feel something." This sentiment echoes across many young musicians who have found solace, inspiration, and validation in Swift's music and journey.

So, what's the learning here in the context of our book title, "Shake it Off – The Taylor Swift Way of Standing Tall and Staying Real in a Shaky World?" It's about the ripple effect of authenticity and resilience. Swift's unwavering commitment to her artistry, despite the many challenges she's faced, is a testament to her strength. She has effectively shaken off the pressures of the industry, standing tall and true to her values and, in doing so, is shaping the future of music by inspiring and influencing young artists.

Take Olivia Rodrigo, for instance. The young star has often cited Swift as one of her most significant influences. In a 2021 interview with NME, Rodrigo said, "I think songwriting is the biggest thing I've taken from her. The way she's able to make such a specific, detailed story and make it a song that everybody can relate to is really inspiring to me."

Swift's reach extends beyond her music. She has consistently used her platform to address social issues, setting a powerful example for young artists to follow. Her advocacy for voting during the 2018 midterm elections was a noteworthy instance of this. Speaking at the American Music Awards, Swift said, "You know what else is voted on by the people? The midterm elections. Please, get out and vote."

Wrapping up Chapter 27, we find that Taylor Swift's legacy is profoundly significant, not just for her record-breaking success and longevity, but for her unwavering commitment to authenticity and her influential role for young artists worldwide. Her legacy is about more than music—it's about being true to oneself, standing tall amidst adversity, and shaking off the pressures of a shaky world.

Her impact on young artists reinforces one of our powerful principles: Authenticity can inspire change. In her actions, Taylor Swift shows us how one can remain true to themselves and their values while making a significant impact in their field. It's a lesson we can all take to heart.

Chapter 28

The Power of Song: Taylor's Impact on Her Fans

In the glittering world of music and fame, Taylor Swift has built an unbreakable connection with her fans. Her songs, filled with raw emotion and personal experiences, have touched millions worldwide, transforming her from a talented artist to an unforgettable companion in her fans' lives.

One might wonder what is so distinctive about Swift's relationship with her fans, often referred to as "Swifties". The answer lies in the heart of her music. Taylor's songs, marked by honesty and authenticity, allow fans to connect with her on an incredibly personal level.

From teenage heartbreaks captured in "Love Story" to poignant reflections of maturity in "Folklore", Swift has a knack for penning down emotions that resonate with her fans. These stories, some of aching heartbreak and others of enduring love, not only reflect Taylor's journey but also echo the experiences of her fans.

Swift's unique ability to share her life through her music has allowed her to connect deeply with her fans. She said it best during an interview with CBS in 2014, "I've taken the approach that I'm just honest with everyone. I want the fans to know that I'm not going to look at them and lie."

Her concerts and interactions with fans further testify to her genuine care and appreciation for them. Swift's tradition of "Secret Sessions" shows her dedication to her fans. She's been known to spend hours connecting with fans, proving that to Taylor, each fan is more than just a face in the crowd.

One such story that stands out is of a fan named Rebekah who was struggling financially. Swift, upon hearing her story, sent her a cheque of $1,989 to help out with her student loans. Swift's personal note to Rebekah said, "Rebekah, now you're $1,989 closer to paying off those student loans." This beautiful gesture showcases not just Swift's generosity but her sincere empathy for her fans' struggles.

Despite being one of the most successful artists in the world, Swift has managed to maintain a sense of closeness with her fans. In her words during a 2019 concert in Paris, "I've had several upheavals in my life, and the one thing I've always had, every single time, was you... You've always been there for me."

One of the fascinating aspects of Swift's connection with her fans is the transformative power of her songs. She turns her experiences into universal narratives, allowing fans to see themselves in her lyrics. A significant example of this is her song, "Fifteen". Swift narrates her experiences as a teenager, capturing feelings of vulnerability and growth. She told MTV in 2009, "I wrote this song about the fact that I'm now 19, looking back on when I was introduced to the concept of popularity and the social hierarchy of high school."

There is also a deep sense of empathy in Swift's music, which fans find comforting. She sings about heartbreak, betrayal, joy, and love - emotions that everyone experiences at some point. It's her bravery in sharing these raw emotions and personal stories that endear her to her fans. Swift once said at the iHeartRadio Music Awards in 2015, "I want you to know that for me, the idea of looking out into an endless sea of crowd that was all jumping and dancing — the only thing that's important to me — are the individual people in the room."

What's more, Swift has shown that she genuinely cares for her fans. In the face of the COVID-19 pandemic, Swift cancelled her 2020 tour dates, prioritizing the health of her fans. She posted on Twitter, "I'm so sad I won't be able to see you guys in concert this year, but I know this is the right decision. Please, please stay healthy and safe."

Wrapping up Chapter 28, we've glimpsed the beautiful bond between Taylor Swift and her fans, a testament to the power of her music. Swift's willingness to bare her soul through her songs and her genuine appreciation for her fans' support are key to this enduring relationship.

Herein lies another powerful principle: Authenticity creates deep connections. Taylor Swift's impact on her fans teaches us the power of being true to oneself and connecting with others through shared experiences. It's a lesson we can carry into our own lives, reminding us to stay real, even in a shaky world.

Chapter 29

Embracing Change: Swift's Journey to Authenticity

Taylor Swift has embraced change throughout her life and career, transforming from a budding country singer to an international pop star, all while staying true to herself.

Taylor's ability to embrace change while remaining authentic is evident in her music's evolution. She began her career with a strong country aesthetic in her self-titled debut album, "Taylor Swift." But as her experiences widened and her creative vision evolved, so did her music. Her gradual shift to pop, culminating in the release of the album "1989," was a bold move. Many fans and critics questioned this change, but Taylor stood by her decision. At the 2015 Grammy Awards, she famously stated, "I wouldn't be the artist I am today without Nashville. It's so amazing to have changed genre and still feel so much love from the Country community."

But Taylor's journey to authenticity isn't limited to her music. It's also about how she's managed to stay real in a world that's constantly scrutinizing her. She's weathered criticisms, feuds, heartbreaks, and much more, but instead of letting these experiences silence her, she's used them to strengthen her voice. A perfect example is her album "Reputation," which served as her statement against the media's portrayal of her.

Also noteworthy is her fight for artists' rights, standing up against music industry giants to ensure fair pay and recognition for all artists. She noted in her Billboard Woman of the Decade speech in 2019, "The definition of the toxic male privilege in our industry is people saying 'but he's always been nice to me'... Well, OF COURSE he's nice to you. If you're in this room, you have something he needs."

An essential part of her journey to authenticity was learning to shake off external expectations. Taylor once said in a 2020 Variety interview, "I don't think people understand how easy it is to infer that someone who's a female artist or a female in our industry is somehow doing something wrong by wanting love, wanting money, wanting success. Women are not allowed to want those things the way that men are allowed to want them." In embracing change, Taylor has learned to pursue her desires, ignoring societal pressures and unfair judgments.

Taylor's transition to pop was a significant turning point in her career, marking her readiness to explore uncharted territories. But the change wasn't only about switching genres; it was a commitment to personal growth and creative exploration. This evolution shows that Taylor wasn't afraid of being different or trying something new. Her willingness to embrace change in her music is a testament to her authenticity and a core principle that has steered her journey so far.

It is evident that Taylor's approach to change is not about discarding her past or disregarding her roots. Instead, she values the experiences that have shaped her, cherishes her beginnings, and carries those lessons forward as she charts her path. As Taylor herself said in her acceptance speech at the 2019 American Music Awards, "All any of the artists in this room want is to create something that will last. The fact that this is an award that celebrates a decade of hard work and art and fun and memories, all that matters to me is the memories that I've had with you guys, with the fans, over the years."

In conclusion, reinforces the principle of embracing change while staying true to oneself. Swift's journey to authenticity is a testimony to her ability to adapt, evolve, and remain rooted in her true self amidst the changes. It's about standing tall, shaking off the dust, and marching forward, a lesson for all of us.

The heartening lesson from this chapter is clear – change is an inevitable part of life. As Swift's journey demonstrates, it is not about resisting these changes, but about embracing them and using them as an opportunity to grow, evolve, and stay true to ourselves.

Chapter 30

The Personal Growth: Taylor's Journey of Self-Discovery

The heart of Taylor Swift's journey - her path to self-discovery and personal growth. It's a journey marked by vulnerability, strength, and the kind of resilience that's only forged through life's many trials and tribulations.

From the moment Taylor Swift stepped into the limelight, her life became an open book. Her experiences, heartbreaks, victories, and personal revelations are encoded in the lyrics of her songs, providing a glimpse into her growth. However, the journey to self-discovery is rarely a straightforward one; it's a winding road filled with challenges, introspection, and learning.

One significant aspect of Taylor's self-discovery journey is her growth in understanding love. In her early career, Taylor's songs painted a fairy-tale-like picture of love. As she matured, so did her songs, which began to reflect a more nuanced understanding of love. In an interview with Rolling Stone in 2014, Taylor shared, "I used to think that I could figure out some pattern of relationships, and it's just not possible. You can't make rules about love."

Taylor's journey also saw her becoming more politically vocal, a step that took courage and conviction. In the past, she had largely kept her political views to herself. But in 2018, Swift broke her silence with an Instagram post encouraging her followers to vote in the upcoming midterm elections. She wrote, "In the past, I've been reluctant to publicly voice my political opinions, but due to several events in my life and in the world in the past two years, I feel very differently about that now."

The aspect of her personal growth that truly stands out is her self-love journey. Taylor has always been candid about her struggles with body image and the pressure to fit into the 'pop star mold.' But in recent years, she's learned to embrace herself, imperfections and all. In a Netflix documentary, 'Miss Americana,' she shared, "I want to wear pink and tell you how I feel about politics, and I don't think that those things have to cancel each other out."

In her quest for self-discovery, Taylor has also learned the power of saying no and setting boundaries, as evident in her battle for her masters' rights. Taylor has shown us that standing up for oneself is a crucial part of personal growth and self-discovery.

In her relationship with actor Joe Alwyn, Taylor has found a more private kind of love, one that she has fiercely protected from the public eye, marking another significant step in her journey towards self-discovery and maturity. During an acceptance speech at the iHeartRadio Music Awards in 2019, she said, "When there's new music, you'll be the first to know." This statement marked a new chapter of self-discovery, where she decided to take control of her narrative.

In conclusion, Taylor Swift's journey of self-discovery is a testament to her strength and resilience. Her personal growth is a lesson that it's okay to make mistakes, change, and grow. As she navigates through her life with grace and conviction, she teaches us the value of authenticity, the courage of standing up for what we believe in, and the beauty of personal evolution.

On the journey to self-discovery, Taylor also learned to weather criticism and controversy. "When you're living for the approval of strangers, and that is where you derive all of your joy and fulfillment, one bad thing can cause everything to crumble," Swift reflected in an interview with CBS Sunday Morning in 2019. She learned to rely less on external validation, discovering her worth from within.

Chapter 31

The Struggle Behind the Spotlight: Taylor's Trials and Triumphs

There's an old saying that goes, "Heavy is the head that wears the crown." This couldn't be truer for global superstars like Taylor Swift. Despite her countless awards, record-breaking hits, and a strong fan base, Taylor's journey has been speckled with trials that tested her strength and resilience.

Taylor's initial rise to fame was meteoric. The release of her debut album at just 16 brought her into the international spotlight. The enormous success of hits like "Love Story" and "You Belong with Me" seemed to promise a smooth path ahead, but there were stormy seas lurking behind the horizon.

In an interview with Rolling Stone in 2019, Taylor expressed, "The stuff that hurts you is the stuff that makes you doubt the things that you believed were always true, and makes you question your abilities". A string of highly publicized relationships and breakups, media scrutiny, a high-profile feud with Kanye West and Kim Kardashian, and legal disputes with her former record label, Big Machine Label Group, cast long shadows over her dazzling success.

But the struggles didn't break Taylor; they made her stronger. Her album 'Reputation', released in 2017, showcased a more mature and self-assured Taylor. She addressed the controversies head-on, using her music as her most powerful weapon. The album sold 1.2 million copies in its first week, proving her resilience and the loyalty of her fans.

And then came an unexpected trial - her mother, Andrea Swift, was diagnosed with cancer. The news hit Taylor hard, but she channeled her pain into music, penning the emotional track "Soon You'll Get Better" in her album 'Lover' as a tribute to her mother's courage.

Despite the hurdles, Taylor's spirit remained unbroken. During her acceptance speech at the 2019 American Music Awards, where she won the Artist of the Decade Award, she said, "All any of the artists, or really anyone in this room, wants is to create something that will last. And all you want to do is create something that will last," illustrating her undying commitment to her craft.

A significant trial that Taylor faced was a tumultuous feud with music mogul Scooter Braun, who acquired her music catalog without her consent in 2019. This battle was a profound shock to Taylor, a cruel reminder of the unsavory aspects of the music industry. It threatened to shake her foundation. Swift was vocal about this struggle, stating in a Tumblr post, "This is my worst case scenario." The pain and frustration were real, but true to her nature, Taylor didn't let this hardship take her down.

During her acceptance speech at the Billboard Women in Music event in 2019, Taylor made an impassioned plea about artists' rights. She stated, "The definition of the toxic male privilege in our industry is people saying, 'but he's always been nice to me' when I'm raising valid concerns about artists and their rights to own their music." This quote perfectly encapsulates how she used her platform to stand up against injustices in the music industry.

She didn't just survive her trials, she emerged from them stronger, more authentic, and more determined. In a heartfelt letter to her fans during this turbulent time, Taylor wrote, "It's been a long time coming, but I've finally learned that the 'Shake It Off' approach isn't about dismissing the pain or the problems we face. It's about dealing with them head-on, about standing tall and staying true to who we are, even when the world seems to be against us."

In wrapping up this chapter, Taylor's trials and triumphs remind us that everyone, even the biggest stars, faces their own battles. The spotlight may shine brightly, but it casts dark shadows. Taylor's approach to these trials, however, illuminates the essence of the "Shake It Off" mantra: standing tall and staying true to oneself, even when the world seems to shake under your feet. Her story encourages us to face our own struggles with courage, to channel pain into strength, and to remember that every setback can set us up for a comeback.

Chapter 32

Through the Looking Glass: A Closer Look at Taylor's World

Taylor Swift is not just a music icon; she's also a unique personality whose world extends beyond the recording studio and the concert stage. In this chapter, we venture deeper into her personal life, giving you a glimpse of Taylor's world beyond her career.

Taylor's love for cats is legendary. Meredith Grey and Olivia Benson, her beloved Scottish Fold cats, are named after her favorite TV characters. This is a fun side of Taylor, showing her light-heartedness and relatability. Once, she told TIME magazine, "The weirdest thing about having cats is that they have wild instincts but live indoors. They're like mini, more-adorable lions." This quote reflects her quirky sense of humor and genuine love for her pets.

Her philanthropic spirit also shines bright. Taylor has often used her platform to contribute to causes close to her heart. From donating to disaster relief efforts to helping fund education, she has proven that her world involves much more than just music. Taylor once said at a charity event in 2019, "You have the ability to change someone's life with a simple act of kindness."

Taylor's creativity extends beyond music into the realm of fashion. She's become a style icon, often seen sporting a mix of vintage and modern styles that have become her signature look. In a 2020 interview with Vogue, she shared, "Fashion is all about self-expression and creativity. Just like music, it's a way for me to tell my story." This authentic approach to style is another aspect of how Taylor shares her personality with the world.

Taylor's world is also filled with her friends, lovingly referred to as the "Squad." From Selena Gomez to Ed Sheeran, Taylor values her friendships greatly. In a 2017 interview with Rolling Stone, she said, "My friends are the kind of people that have their own lives, and their own busy schedules, and that's why we get along so well."

To sum up, Taylor's world is a blend of her love for music, cats, fashion, friendships, and philanthropy. Despite her fame, she has stayed true to her values and herself, constantly proving that being real is the best way to stand tall in a shaky world. We learn that the Taylor Swift way isn't about brushing off life's challenges. Instead, it's about embracing them with authenticity and turning them into stepping stones for personal growth. As we take a closer look at her world, we see a picture of a woman who is more than her music - she's a beacon of authenticity and resilience.

Taylor's sense of humor is another key element that defines her world. Despite the hardships and challenges, she never loses her ability to laugh at herself. We've seen this repeatedly, from her light-hearted music videos to her entertaining social media posts. She once told a crowd at her 'Lover' concert in 2019, "In my world, it's okay to make fun of yourself. Laughter really is the best medicine."

Music, of course, is the beating heart of Taylor's world. It is her emotional outlet, her comfort, her tool for storytelling, and her medium of connection with her fans. Her passion for music started at a young age, and she hasn't wavered from it despite all the challenges and transformations in her life. In an interview with Billboard in 2020, she said, "Music is not just what I do, it's who I am. It's my way of understanding the world and expressing myself within it."

Wrapping up, this intimate peek into Taylor's world uncovers her relatable, multifaceted, and down-to-earth nature. Despite the glamorous life that fame brought her, she has maintained a strong connection to the things that truly matter: her love for music, her relationships with her fans and loved ones, her passion for philanthropy, and her quirky sense of humor. This chapter teaches us that in order to 'shake it off' and stand tall, it's crucial to stay grounded and connected to what genuinely matters. The strength to persevere comes from an authentic place, and that's what makes Taylor Swift a true inspiration.

Chapter 33

The Quiet Strength: Taylor's Path to Inner Peace

In the bustling world of fame and glitter, Taylor Swift stands as a testament to the power of inner peace. Despite the enormous pressures and expectations that come with her celebrity status, Taylor has found a way to keep her calm, demonstrating a quiet strength that continues to inspire her fans worldwide.

Swift's journey to inner peace has been anything but smooth. It's been a whirlwind of heartbreaks, betrayals, public scrutiny, and personal battles. However, it's also been a journey of learning, growing, and evolving. She once confessed in an interview with Vogue in 2019, "I've learned that you have to make peace with the fact that not everyone is going to love what you do. The important thing is that you love what you do."

Her songs have been an essential part of her path to inner peace, serving as emotional outlets. Music has been her therapy, a place for her to process her feelings and find a sense of peace. As she said in her acceptance speech for Billboard's Woman of the Decade in 2019, "I've learned that my work, my music, is my way of dealing with my emotions. It's my way of finding peace."

Another key to Swift's inner peace is her prioritization of personal relationships over public opinions. She values her close relationships – her family, her friends, her fans – far more than the critics' approval. This shift in focus helps her stay grounded and provides a buffer against the often harsh world of celebrity. During an Instagram live session in 2020, Taylor shared, "At the end of the day, the people who matter are the ones who are there for you. They're the ones who bring you peace."

Taking time for herself and her interests outside of music also plays a crucial role in her journey. Whether it's baking cookies, writing poetry, or spending time with her beloved cats, these moments of solitude and simple joys help Taylor recharge and find a sense of balance in her life.

The essence of Taylor Swift's quiet strength is found in her self-awareness and emotional resilience. She has faced criticism, judgment, and intrusion into her personal life, and yet, she has managed to stay focused, grounded, and authentic to herself. This journey towards inner peace didn't happen overnight; it's a culmination of moments, experiences, lessons, and decisions

One such moment came during the 2016 Grammy Awards, where she won Album of the Year for "1989". In her acceptance speech, she shared a powerful message, "As the first woman to win Album of the Year at the Grammys twice, I want to say to all the young women out there, there are going to be people along the way who will try to undercut your success or take credit for your accomplishments or your fame... but if you just focus on the work and you don't let those people sidetrack you, someday when you get where you're going, you'll look around and you will know that it was you and the people who love you who put you there. And that will be the greatest feeling in the world." This statement was a clear reflection of her quiet strength and inner peace, rooted in her work and the support of those who truly care for her.

In conclusion, Taylor Swift's journey to inner peace is a testament to her resilience, strength, and the power of focusing on what truly matters. It's a lesson in shaking off external pressures and standing tall in the face of adversity. As we close this chapter, we realize that Taylor's journey to inner peace is a vivid example of staying real in a shaky world. It reminds us that inner peace comes from authenticity, personal growth, and a relentless focus on the things that truly matter.

Chapter 34

Learning to "Shake it Off": Turning Negatives into Positives

As we reach the final chapter of our journey exploring Taylor Swift's remarkable life and career, we've saved one of the most important principles for last: the ability to "Shake it Off". In life, we all encounter hardships, criticisms, and negativity. Taylor, living her life in the public eye, has faced more than her fair share. Yet, she has consistently demonstrated an exceptional knack for transforming negatives into positives, turning setbacks into comebacks.

Perhaps the most iconic example of this is her 2014 hit single, "Shake It Off". When the world seemed intent on focusing on her personal life, Taylor addressed it head-on with a catchy tune and infectious dance beats. The message? She wasn't going to let negativity get her down; she was going to "shake it off". In an interview with Rolling Stone magazine in 2014, she expressed, "The message in 'Shake It Off' is a problem we all deal with, an issue we deal with on a daily basis — we don't live just in a celebrity takedown culture, we live in a takedown culture. People will find anything about you and twist it to where it's weird or wrong or annoying or strange or bad. You have to not only live your life in spite of people who don't understand you — you have to have more fun than they do."

The way Taylor dealt with the controversy around her master recordings in 2019 is another testament to her philosophy. When Scooter Braun's Ithaca Holdings acquired her former label Big Machine Label Group and, with it, the masters of her first six albums, she was initially heartbroken. She took to social media to express her feelings, and then? She announced plans to re-record her old music, thereby reclaiming control over her work. It was a defiant and inspiring move that turned a potential setback into a positive new chapter.

In a speech at Elle's 2019 Women in Music event, Taylor shared this sentiment: "We have to live bravely in order to truly feel alive, and that means not being ruled by our greatest fears." By turning negativity into positivity, Taylor has shown us how to live bravely, even in the face of adversity.

As we look at Swift's career and her relationship with her fans, it's evident that this attitude has not just been crucial to her success, but also influential to those who look up to her. There is no doubt that every heartbreak, every hurdle, every feud, has been translated into her music, and instead of casting a shadow, it's been crafted into a beacon of light that shines brighter than any hardship.

In an interview with Vogue in 2019, Swift candidly stated, "There's a different vocabulary for men and women in the music industry. I'll say exactly the same thing as a male artist, but as soon as I say it, it's like 'Oh, she's so calculated. She's manipulating everything.' And I'm like, no, I'm just telling you what happened."

As we conclude this chapter, and indeed this book, we're reminded of the powerful lessons Taylor Swift offers us all. From shaking off negativity to standing tall in the face of adversity, her approach to life is both inspirational and profoundly empowering. These principles don't just apply to superstars; they're lessons we can all take to heart. So, as Taylor Swift herself might say: when the world gets shaky, remember to stand tall, stay real, and always, always shake it off.

"Shake it Off", both the song and the mantra, is much more than a catchy tune. It's a testament to Swift's resilience, her strength, and her tenacity. It's a clear illustration of how she navigates the music industry, and the world at large, turning adversity into opportunity and refocusing negative energy into her work, creating music that resonates with millions

Afterword

And there you have it - an intimate journey through the life of a star who has been a beacon of resilience and authenticity, a woman who continuously teaches us the power of standing tall and staying real in a shaky world: Taylor Swift.

As you close this book, the melodies of her life story continue to resonate. We hope it has inspired you, taught you, and sparked something within you - much like her music does. Perhaps it has revealed a side of Taylor that you didn't know before, or reinforced why you admired her in the first place. Maybe it has shown you the importance of staying true to oneself in the face of adversity and challenges.

But the journey doesn't stop here. Every story has the power to influence, and Taylor's is no exception. This is a story that deserves to be shared, an experience that should be passed on.

Think about the young women in your life - friends, daughters, sisters, or students. Imagine what it might mean for them to read this account of a woman who has stood tall despite her shaky surroundings, who has shaken off the critics and haters to remain undeniably herself. It's a reminder for all of us that even in the face of seemingly insurmountable challenges, we have the strength to rise and shine.

So, consider passing this book along, or gifting a copy to someone who might need to hear Taylor's story. Let it inspire others as it has inspired you. Because when it comes to stories of resilience, strength, and authenticity - much like the lessons in our favorite songs - they are meant to be shared and cherished.

Thank you for being a part of this journey. Just remember, when life gets too shaky, channel your inner Taylor and 'Shake it Off'.

Made in United States
Troutdale, OR
09/07/2023

12704104R00066